Royal Doulton
A Legacy of Excellence
1871-1945

Gregg Whittecar & Arron Rimpley

4880 Lower Valley Road, Atglen, PA 19310 USA

Library of Congress Cataloging-in-Publication Data

Whittecar, Gregg.
  Royal Doulton : a legacy of excellence 1871-1945 / by Gregg
Whittecar & Arron Rimpley.
     p. cm.
  ISBN 0-7643-1797-0
1. Doulton and Company--Catalogs. 2. Pottery, English--Catalogs. I.
Rimpley, Arron. II. Title.
NK4210.D65W57 2003
738'.09424'63075--dc21

                          2002156715

Title page photo: John Eyre tile panel, 1887

Designed by Mark David Bowyer
Type set in Korinna BT

ISBN: 0-7643-1797-0
Printed in China
1 2 3 4

Published by Schiffer Publishing Ltd.
4880 Lower Valley Road
Atglen, PA 19310
Phone: (610) 593-1777; Fax: (610) 593-2002
E-mail: Info@schifferbooks.com
Please visit our web site catalog at **www.schifferbooks.com**
We are always looking for people to write books on new and
related subjects. If you have an idea for a book please contact us
at the above address.

This book may be purchased from the publisher.
Include $3.95 for shipping. Please try your bookstore first.
You may write for a free catalog.

In Europe, Schiffer books are distributed by
Bushwood Books
6 Marksbury Ave.
Kew Gardens
Surrey TW9 4JF England
Phone: 44 (0) 20 8392-8585; Fax: 44 (0) 20 8392-9876
E-mail: Bushwd@aol.com
Free postage in the U.K., Europe; air mail at cost.

Contents

An early Doulton and Company advertisement for decorative stoneware pieces.

Acknowledgments

When our new friends at Schiffer Publishing approached us to write this book, we had no idea what an exciting year it would be for us! We have traveled the world to research and photograph artistic treasures from Doulton's Lambeth and Burslem studios. It was our pleasure to spend time with collectors and experts on both sides of the Atlantic who were willing to share their extraordinary pieces and vast knowledge with us and our readers. Collectors of Royal Doulton and connoisseurs of art pottery will appreciate this opportunity to view many pieces never before seen.

We are greatly indebted to everyone who provided hands-on assistance, as well as those whose previous research contributed to the production of this book. Although many remain unacknowledged due to time and space constraints, without their invaluable help our book would not have been possible. We extend our special thanks to the following people:

Joanne Geary, our dear friend and Director of Operations at the Whitley Collection, spent countless hours measuring, identifying, and cataloging over 1,400 art ware pieces for the book. Researching in England, Joanne explored the dusty Doulton archives where she discovered a daily diary kept by George Tinworth's wife — a treasure never before uncovered. She also found two sketchbooks by Hannah Barlow with numerous drawings and watercolors. These sketchbooks, like the diary, had been long forgotten. It is our hope that Joanne's discoveries will one day be published for all Doulton collectors to enjoy.

Joan Jones, author and curator of both the Royal Doulton Museum Archives and those at Minton, was kind enough to write the foreword to our publication. She coordinated our visit to the Royal Doulton archives and helped us in our search for photographic treasures to add to this book.

Jocelyn Lukins, a respected journalist and professional photographer, as well as a dealer of Royal Doulton wares, lent her support, research, and expertise to this project. She read our original copy for historical accuracy making many humorous comments and helpful suggestions. Ms. Lukins allowed us access to her archived photographs for selections used in our publication.

Louise Irvine, an international lecturer and author, is known as a treasure trove of fascinating facts and stories about all things Doulton. As she continuously shares her research through lectures and publications, she inspires thousands of collectors both new and old.

Jean Tittle, a collector and friend, edited our copy and helped bring the Doulton story to life. Her thirty-one years of teaching high school English proved invaluable. As 1997 Creative Writing Teacher of the Year in Michigan, honor graduates frequently selected her as most significant educator at her school.

The late Desmond Eyles spent years researching the original Doulton story. He wrote much of the information dealers and collectors enjoy today. Any author of a book on Doulton is indebted to Mr. Eyles.

Geoffrey Bridgwood, staff photographer for the Royal Doulton Museums and Archives, shared his expertise in photographing historic pictures, including taking pictures from glass slides.

Michael Matarazzo, a collector and a professional photographer assisted with our photo shoots in New York. Our portraits on the book jacket are examples of Michael's professional talent.

Last, but certainly not least, our friends and valued collectors listed below graciously opened their homes and allowed us to photograph their collections. Their hospitality was appreciated, their enthusiasm for our project was contagious, and their art wares are some of the finest in the world.

Terry Anderson and Jim Napoleon
David and Sheila Bearman
Gary Burlin and Harold Bemis
Howard and Rosemarie Eskin
Donald and Diane Kendall, Jr.
Michael Matarazzo
Allan and Candace Shanks
Arthur and Paulette Wiener
Harry and Erla Zuber

It is our hope that you enjoy this book as much as we enjoyed bringing together these examples of Doulton's Legacy of Excellence.

Gregg Whittecar and Arron Rimpley
Spring, 2003

Engraving of Doulton offices and studios built in 1876-77 at High Street, Lambeth.

Foreword

There can never be enough books illustrating the diversity of Royal Doulton productions. This book, intended to be a publication for pure enjoyment, provides the Doulton enthusiast with a privileged view into some of the most exclusive private collections of Doulton in the United States.

Its publication enables us to see these treasured Doulton pieces, which have been collected over the years, and which have now been collated and made available to us for the first time — the book is a veritable feast of sheer exuberance of modeling and decoration from Doulton. For lovers of Lambeth wares the most talented artists and sculptors are well represented and the not-so-well known are introduced to us. Bold and freely painted Lambeth Faience contrasts with the more delicately painted and raised gilded pieces from the Burslem Studio. Figure enthusiasts have not been forgotten – rare Vellum figures are well represented – and the unique Doulton experimental glazes of Flambé and Titanian feature strongly. A visually stimulating book, *Royal Doulton: A Legacy of Excellence 1871-1945* will inspire and encourage the Doulton collector in all of us.

Joan Jones
Royal Doulton Museums Curator

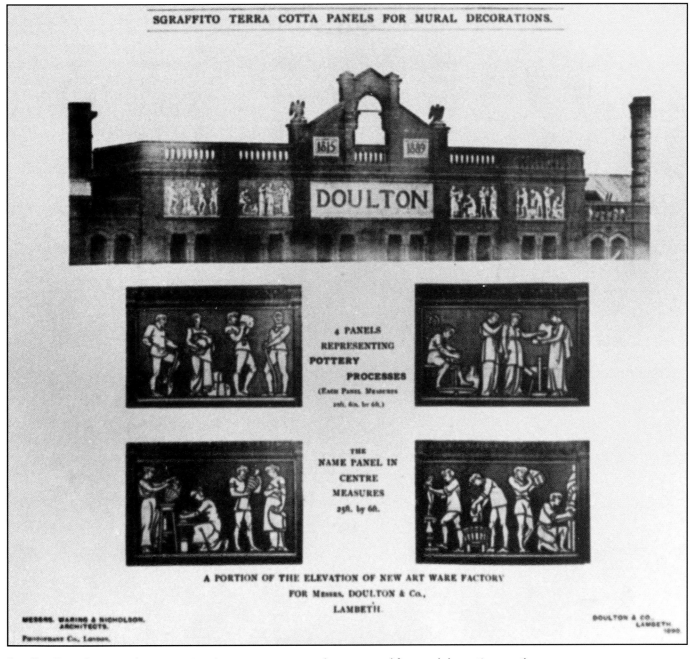

Sgraffito Terra Cotta panels representing the pottery processes that were used for mural decorations on the new art ware factory built for Doulton and Company. The top picture shows the front elevation of the new factory.

Doulton Lambeth

I n 1815, as Napoleon Bonaparte suffered defeat at Waterloo, John Doulton, age 22, invested his life savings of £100 in a small riverside pottery in Lambeth on the south bank of the Thames. Previously having worked for the widow Mrs. Martha Jones at her Vauxhall Walk Pottery, John became a partner with Mrs. Jones and her foreman John Watts.

John Doulton, 1793-1873. Founder of the company.

One of 170 in the area, their pottery produced utilitarian salt-glazed stoneware. When Mrs. Jones retired in 1820, the company was renamed Doulton and Watts. It soon became one of the most important potteries in Lambeth. Today it is world renowned as the Royal Doulton Company whose products are the hallmark of excellence in ceramic art.

Early production from Doulton and Watts included salt-glazed stoneware bottles, jars, and other packaging containers. Soon brown figure mugs and jugs in the likeness of Nelson and other contemporary politicians and royals were in vogue. Next came commemorative wares in the salt-glazed stoneware. Among the rarest of these are the "Reform" bottles and flasks made in 1832 to celebrate the passing of the first Reform Act. These early bottles and flasks were the predecessors of a later series of stoneware commemorative figures, busts, flasks, and jugs, which are rare and highly collectible in today's market.

The Doulton family tradition was firmly established in 1835 when John Doulton's son, Henry, expressed his desire to join his father and his older brother John at what was now called Lambeth Pottery. Under his father's guidance, Henry started an informal yet strict apprenticeship. He was granted no favors or privileges and had to learn every aspect of the potter's craft, from preparing the clays and other raw materials to firing and salting the wares. Through Henry's dedication and personal ambition, he acquired full knowledge of the pottery trade, allowing him to play a leading role in the day-to-day operation of the pottery.

Sir Henry Doulton, 1820-1897.

In the early part of his career, Henry Doulton concentrated on the development and perfection of industrial ceramics used by engineers, architects, and builders. In the late 1840s, Henry turned his attention to sanitation. An intelligent and ambitious entrepreneur, Henry anticipated the sanitary revolution's financial potential as London and the new industrial cities began construction of modern sewer and water systems.

Lambeth Pottery initiated large-scale production of stoneware drainpipes and related wares. Their timing was perfect and Lambeth products were soon being installed beneath the streets of London and other cities. Henry Doulton's foresight not only benefited the company, but the Doulton family as well. Ironically, the future of Royal Doulton's reputation for excellence was built on these unromantic yet vital wares. Many of the sewer and water pipes they made are still in use today.

Opposite page:
Doulton's display of stoneware at the
Philadelphia Centennial Exhibition, 1876.

Thanks in large part to the sanitary revolution, the name and reputation of the Doulton Company spread the world over. The pottery also began displaying its wares at international exhibitions, further increasing the company's reputation and gaining attention outside the ceramic industry.

In the 1860s, Henry became interested in the creative endeavors taking place at the Lambeth School of Art. Persuaded by John Sparkes, principal of the school, Henry Doulton employed a few students on an experimental basis. The first students produced their rather simple pieces at the art school, which were then fired at the Doulton factory. These early studio wares, art pots, vases in blue and white, and spirit flasks were enthusiastically received at the Paris Exhibition of 1867 and the International Exhibition of London in 1871.

In addition to the impression made on the art critics and the public, the Lambeth wares also attracted the attention of their most important patron, Queen Victoria. The Queen placed orders for pieces to be sent to Windsor Castle and throughout her reign took great interest in the Doulton factory.

William Askew working on his wheel in the Lambeth factory.

Henry Doulton continued to give the Lambeth Studio his full support, thus encouraging its development. England had never seen, nor has ever seen, such a grand scale co-existence between art and industry. Doulton's ceramic wares continued to be shown at one great exhibition after another, taking the highest awards.

By the time of the Philadelphia Exhibition in 1876, close to 1,500 pieces of Doulton ware were shown, a remarkable achievement since five years earlier only seventy pieces had been displayed at the London Exhibition. At the Paris Exhibition in 1878, Henry Doulton was honored the Grand Prix—the highest honor ever awarded to any pottery. Within a span of twelve years the Doulton wares, beginning in a small corner of the Lambeth Pottery, had become a major force in the revival of English pottery.

The significance of the studio was not only in its products, but the effect it had on the entire ceramic industry. The Lambeth experience encouraged all potteries throughout Britain to start art departments. This new philosophy enhanced the prestige of British ceramics around the world. Doulton and other great manufacturers of the period such as Minton, George Jones, and Copeland achieved a position of world dominance.

Henry Doulton was determined that each artist be given free rein to experiment and develop his or her own unique style. He created an artistic environment where no official guidelines had to be followed. The leading artists from the Art Studio were George Tinworth, Mark V. Marshall, Frank A. Butler and members of the Barlow family, Hannah, Arthur and Florence.

Doulton employee Jimmy Speer standing in front of his horse-drawn delivery van, c. 1905.

A painting by Thomas Wakeman of the Doulton and Watts Pottery, High Street, Lambeth, c. 1840.

George Tinworth (1866 – 1913)

From first joining the Lambeth Pottery in 1866 until his death in 1913, George Tinworth was Doulton's premier artist, visited and admired by the leading figures of the day, including British Royalty. Tinworth is best known today for his whimsical small-scale models of mice and frogs. However, during his lifetime he was better known for his religious sculptures and relief panels, often monumental in scale.

Tinworth, the son of a wheelwright, was educated at home by his deeply religious mother. She instructed him in the scriptures, giving him biblical knowledge that would later provide him with inspiration for his terra cotta and statuary work.

In 1866, John Sparkes persuaded Henry Doulton to admit Tinworth, a particularly talented young student from the Lambeth School of Art, to work in his pottery. Tinworth was confined to a small corner of the factory, given a chimney pot on which to sit, a tub on which to balance a modeling board and allowed access to only the clays, glazes and kilns used for the stoneware pipes.

In the beginning, Tinworth designed water filter cases and modeled a number of large terra cotta medallions in a Neo-Classical style. These medallions impressed art critic, John Ruskin, who was instrumental in bringing Tinworth to the attention of the art world. Tinworth soon began decorating stoneware vases and jugs thrown by the factory's potters.

Next, Tinworth developed both a series of sculptural reliefs and decorated vases in salt-glazed stoneware. Using a piece of pointed boxwood, Tinworth etched his designs into pieces still in a soft state. Seaweed vines, scrolls, and leafy forms with beaded runners became his characteristic trademark.

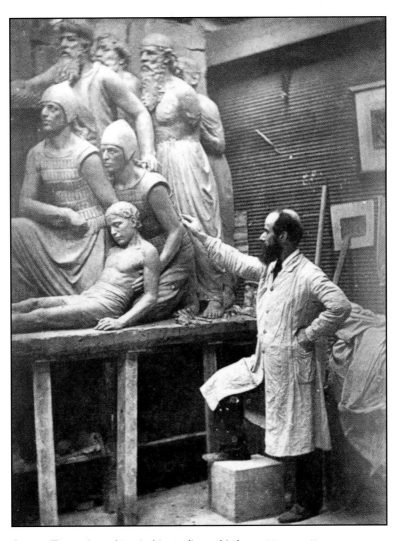

George Tinworth working in his studio on his largest terra cotta panel, *Christ Before Herod*, 1887.

Tinworth's early creations were first exhibited at the 1867 Paris Exhibition where critics praised the innovative developments in English art ceramics. A later exhibition in London proved so popular that the future of Doulton's decorative pottery was assured and the Art Pottery Studio was expanded. By 1881, more than 250 men and women were employed to create stoneware art pieces.

Tinworth concentrated on designing large-scale sculptures and relief panels. Many of his works were produced in salt-glazed stoneware, while others were made in a fine unglazed terra cotta. The quality modeling and emotional intensity Tinworth invested in his work earned him the title "Rembrandt in Terra Cotta." The Doulton Studio received numerous commissions for Tinworth's religious works, including a crucifixion for the main altar of York Minster, which can still be viewed today.

Tinworth remained with Doulton Lambeth until his death in 1913 at the age of seventy. He was on his way to his studio where he was working on his largest sculptural project, *Christ in the Garden of Gethsemane*. Tinworth will be remembered not only for his remarkable contributions to Victorian art, but to sculpture as well.

Opposite page:
Salt-glazed stoneware fountain modeled by George Tinworth in relief around a pyramidal column with scenes from the Old and New Testaments, 1877. The fountain, standing over 6 feet tall and 6 feet in diameter, was first exhibited at the Paris Universal Exhibition of 1878 and then the Worcester Fine Arts Exhibition of 1882.

Stoneware salt depicting the betrayal and crucifixion of Christ, 1871. George Tinworth, artist. Doulton Lambeth backstamp, 3.75". (C)

Maquette miniature model for Doulton doorway, 1878. George Tinworth, artist; John Broad, assistant. 9" x 12". (D)

Terra cotta lunette designed by George Tinworth for Doulton House, 1878. The featured artists include George Tinworth (holding the vase), Hannah Barlow (sitting on the stool with her cat, Tommy, at her feet) and Henry Doulton (sitting).

"Finding of Moses the Law Giver" plaque, c. 1880. George Tinworth, artist. Doulton Lambeth backstamp, 12" x 21". (B)

"David's Law" plaque, c. 1880. George Tinworth, artist.
Doulton Lambeth backstamp, 7" x 13". (*B*)

"The Eagle & The Fox" plaque, c. 1890. George Tinworth,
artist. Doulton Lambeth backstamp, 6" x 6". (*C*)

"Queen of Sheba's Visit to Solomon" plaque, c. 1880. George
Tinworth, artist. Doulton Lambeth backstamp, 9" x 9". (*D*)

"I Will Draw Water" plaque, c. 1885. George Tinworth, artist. Doulton Lambeth backstamp, 6". (C)

Handle jug with putti (angels) shown at the Philadelphia Exposition of 1876, 1875. George Tinworth, artist, 21". (T)

Vase with foliate design, rosettes and silver-mount top, 1879. George Tinworth, artist. Doulton Lambeth backstamp, 13.5". (B)

Seaweed and foliate vase for Philadelphia Exposition, c. 1872. George Tinworth, artist, 15". (E)

Vase with applied rosettes and beads, 1882. George Tinworth, artist. Doulton Lambeth backstamp, 12.25". (B)

Pair of vases with a dark blue background, c. 1897. George Tinworth, artist. Doulton Lambeth England backstamp, 10.75". (C)

Architectural clock shown at 1876
Philadelphia Exposition, 1875.
George Tinworth, artist, 15". (*F*)

Pitcher with beaded swirls and rosettes, c. 1870. George Tinworth, artist, 10.5". (*B*)

Foliate jug with applied flowers, 1875. George Tinworth, artist, 13.5". (*C*)

Lemonade jugs with sterling mounts, 1874. George Tinworth, artist; Emma Martin, assistant, 9.5" and 11.5". (*B*)

Mr. Pickwick figural, c. 1885.
George Tinworth, artist. Doulton
Lambeth backstamp. (C)

Pair of candlesticks with
angels, 1877. George
Tinworth, artist. Doulton
Lambeth backstamp,
7.75". (C)

Tobacco jar with mouse smoking lid, c. 1900.
George Tinworth, artist. Doulton Lambeth
backstamp, 7". (B)

Square inkwell with putti (angels), 1877. George Tinworth, artist; Margaret Aitken, assistant, 4.5". (C)

Flower holder with cherubs riding sea horses, 1878. George Tinworth, artist. Doulton Lambeth backstamp, 4.25". (C)

Cherubs on a sea horse carriage, 1876. George Tinworth, artist. Doulton Lambeth backstamp, 3.5". (C)

Pair of baby study figures, 1880. George Tinworth, artist. Doulton Lambeth backstamp, 4". (C)

Crow & Pitcher inkwell, c. 1880. George Tinworth, artist. Doulton Lambeth backstamp, 5". (D)

Decorated dish with two cherubs, c. 1875. George Tinworth, artist. Doulton Lambeth backstamp, 3". (B)

Child kneeling holding a vase, c. 1885. George Tinworth, artist; Aitken/Newbury, assistants. Doulton Lambeth backstamp, 10" x 9". (D)

Figure of a boy with vase, pair, 1890. George Tinworth, artist; Mary Aitken, assistant. Doulton Lambeth backstamp, 8". (C)

Figure of a girl with tambourine, c. 1880. George Tinworth, artist. Doulton Lambeth backstamp, 9". (C)

Trojan boy menu holder, c. 1885.
George Tinworth, artist. Doulton
Lambeth backstamp,
5". (B)

Mini vase with
children hanging
from sides,
c. 1880.
George
Tinworth, artist.
Doulton Lambeth
backstamp, 5". (C)

Figure of a boy with watermelon, 1885.
George Tinworth, artist. Doulton
Lambeth backstamp, 3.75". (B)

"The Telephone: Good News" figure, c. 1885.
George Tinworth, artist. Doulton Lambeth
backstamp, 4.25". (*C*)

Figure of a boy pulling a barrel, 1880.
George Tinworth, artist. Doulton
Lambeth backstamp, 5". (*D*)

Spill vase: of a boy with two vases, 1885. George Tinworth, artist.
Doulton Lambeth backstamp, 5.25". (*C*)

Figure of a boy holding vases, c. 1885. George Tinworth, artist. Doulton Lambeth backstamp, 5.25". (B)

Two boys holding urn, c. 1885. George Tinworth, artist. Doulton Lambeth backstamp, 5.5". (C)

"Fowl" individual salt holder, c. 1890. George Tinworth, artist. Doulton Lambeth backstamp, 4". (B)

A group of child figure open salts, 1885. George Tinworth, artist. Doulton Lambeth backstamp, 4". (*B* ea.)

Figure of a boy with eagle urn, 1890. George Tinworth, artist. Doulton Carrera backstamp, 5". (*C*)

Group of figures—Carrera Ware "Fire Station," boy holding vases, and an inkwell, c. 1880. George Tinworth, artist. Doulton Lambeth backstamp, 4". (*C*)

Large figural monkey, c. 1890.
George Tinworth, artist. Doulton
Lambeth backstamp,
20". (*T*)

"Scandal," c. 1880.
George Tinworth,
artist. Doulton
Lambeth backstamp,
6". (D)

"Contentment," 1891. George Tinworth, artist.
Doulton Carrera backstamp, 4.75". (C)

Mice on vase with base, 1881. George Tinworth, artist. Doulton Lambeth backstamp, 5.5". (D)

Mouse fob watch holder, 1885. George Tinworth, artist. Doulton Lambeth backstamp, 4.75". (C)

"Playgoers," 1884. George Tinworth, artist. Doulton Lambeth backstamp, 5". (G)

Pair of mice musicians, c. 1880. George
Tinworth, artist. Doulton Lambeth
backstamp, 4" and 4.5". (B)

"The Monkey That Would Be
a King," c. 1882. George
Tinworth, artist. Doulton
Lambeth backstamp, 4". (D)

"Playgoers" group and "The
Waits" group, c. 1880.
George Tinworth, artist.
Doulton Lambeth
backstamp, 5" & 6". (D ea.)

"Potters" menu holder, c. 1879. George Tinworth, artist. Doulton Lambeth backstamp, 4". (*D*)

"The Conjurors" menu holder, c. 1880. George Tinworth, artist. Doulton Lambeth backstamp, 3.75". (*D*)

Pair of mice menu holders, c. 1885. George Tinworth, artist. Doulton Lambeth backstamp, 4". (*C* ea.)

"The Sculptor" menu holder, 1886. George Tinworth, artist. Doulton Lambeth backstamp, 4". (*C*)

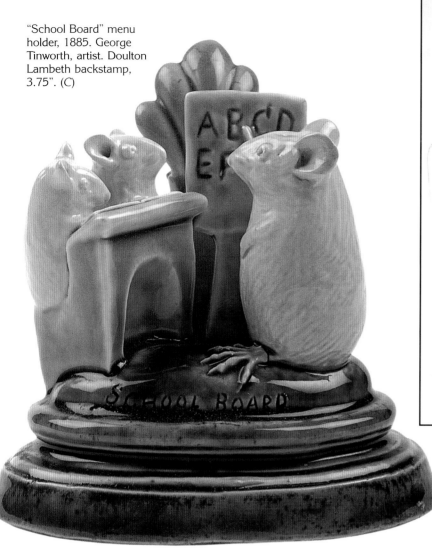

"School Board" menu holder, 1885. George Tinworth, artist. Doulton Lambeth backstamp, 3.75". (C)

Group of mice menu holders, c. 1886. George Tinworth, artist. Doulton Lambeth backstamp, 4". (C ea.)

Trio of mice menu holders, c. 1885. George Tinworth, artist. Doulton Lambeth backstamp, 4.4". (C)

Frog in canoe, c. 1885. George Tinworth, artist. Doulton Lambeth backstamp, 3". (C)

"Drink" mice in their cups, c. 1885. George Tinworth, artist, 3.5". (C)

"Scandal," c. 1885. George Tinworth, artist. Doulton Lambeth backstamp, 4". (C)

"Going to Derby" (two variations), c. 1870. George Tinworth, artist. Doulton Lambeth backstamp, 3.75". (*C* ea.)

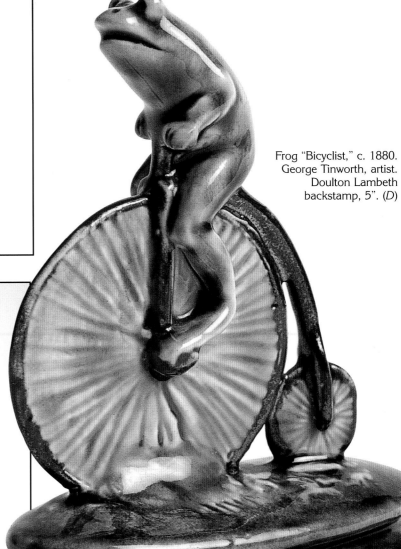

Frog "Bicyclist," c. 1880. George Tinworth, artist. Doulton Lambeth backstamp, 5". (*D*)

"Pillars of Wealth" and "Wheelbarrow" bud vases, c. 1890. George Tinworth, artist. Doulton Lambeth backstamp, 4" and 4.5". (*B*)

"United Family" and "The Frog That Would Be Prince," c. 1870. George Tinworth, artist. Doulton Lambeth backstamp, 4.5". (*D*)

Mouse playing a violin, 1886.
George Tinworth, artist. Doulton
Lambeth backstamp, 4". (B)

"Crossing the Channel,"
c. 1880. George Tinworth, artist.
Doulton Lambeth backstamp, 5". (C)

"The Wheelwright," 1886. George Tinworth,
artist. Doulton Lambeth backstamp, 4". (C)

"The Steeplechase" frog and mouse group, 1886. George Tinworth, artist. Doulton Lambeth backstamp, 4.5". (*G*)

Mouse cornet player, mouse on currant bun, and mouse vase, c. 1884. George Tinworth, artist. Doulton Lambeth backstamp, 3.5". (*C*)

"The Cockneys in Brighton," 1886. George Tinworth, artist. Doulton Lambeth backstamp, 4". (*G*)

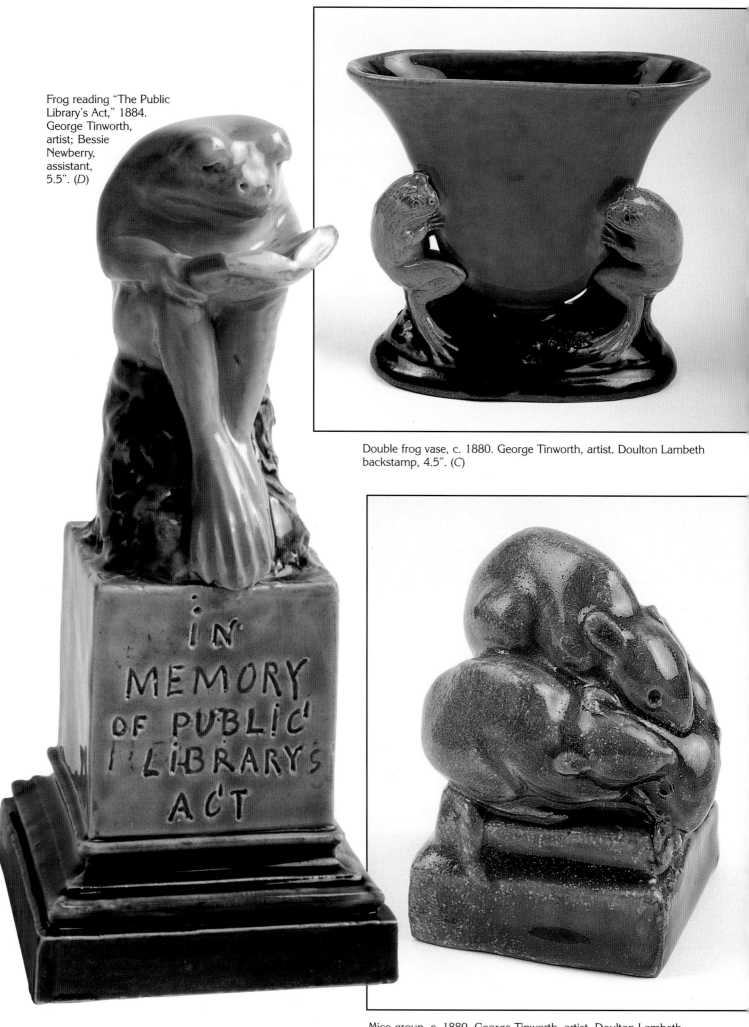

Frog reading "The Public Library's Act," 1884. George Tinworth, artist; Bessie Newberry, assistant, 5.5". (D)

Double frog vase, c. 1880. George Tinworth, artist. Doulton Lambeth backstamp, 4.5". (C)

Mice group, c. 1880. George Tinworth, artist. Doulton Lambeth backstamp, 3". (B)

Musician: boy playing
trumpet,
c. 1890. George
Tinworth, artist.
Doulton Lambeth
backstamp, 4.5". (C)

Musician: One-man band, c. 1890. George Tinworth, artist.
Doulton Lambeth backstamp, 4.75". (C)

A group of merry musicians, c. 1880. George Tinworth, artist. Doulton Lambeth backstamp, 4" (average). (B ea.)

A group of merry
musicians, c. 1880.
George Tinworth, artist.
Doulton Lambeth
backstamp, 4" (aver-
age). (*B* ea.)

Musician: Boy playing
guitar, 1880. George
Tinworth, artist.
Doulton Lambeth
backstamp, 4.5". (*B*)

Musician: Boy playing cello, c. 1880. George Tinworth,
artist. Doulton Lambeth backstamp, 5". (*B*)

A group of merry musicians, c. 1880.
George Tinworth, artist. Doulton Lambeth
backstamp, 4" (average). (*B* ea.)

Musician: Organist, c. 1890.
George Tinworth, artist.
Doulton Lambeth
backstamp, 5". (*C*)

A group of merry
musicians, c. 1880.
George Tinworth,
artist. Doulton
Lambeth
backstamp, 4"
(average). (*B* ea.)

Musician: Boy playing bagpipe, c. 1890. George Tinworth, artist. Doulton Lambeth backstamp, 4.5". (C)

A group of merry musicians, c. 1880. George Tinworth, artist. Doulton Lambeth backstamp, 4" (average). (B ea.)

A group of merry musicians, c. 1880. George Tinworth, artist. Doulton Lambeth backstamp, 4" (average). (B ea.)

A group of merry musicians, c. 1880. George Tinworth, artist. Doulton Lambeth backstamp, 4" (average). (*B* ea.)

Musician: Boy playing mandolin, c. 1890. George Tinworth, artist. Doulton Lambeth backstamp, 3". (*C*)

Musician: Boy playing stringed instrument, c. 1890. George Tinworth, artist. Doulton Lambeth backstamp, 5". (*C*)

A group of merry musicians, c. 1880. George Tinworth, artist. Doulton Lambeth backstamp, 4" (average). (*B* ea.)

The Barlow Family Artists

Hannah (1871-1913)

Hannah (1871-1913)

In 1871, Henry Doulton's new Art Studio employed its first female artist – Hannah Bolton Barlow. Her name eventually became synonymous with the prestigious Lambeth art pottery. Hannah also pioneered the employment of other women in the Lambeth potteries, a field previously dominated by men. Of the nine Barlow children, four were employed at the Lambeth Pottery.

As a small child growing up in the Essex countryside, Hannah Barlow was surrounded by family pets. She expressed her love of these animals in sketches and watercolors, which she filled with life and vigor. Also during her childhood, Hannah watched a potter working on his wheel, sculpting jugs and vases from wet clay. The sight of this "magical transformation" planted the seed for her later career as a ceramic designer.

Hannah, like many of the future employees of the Art Studio, was formally trained at the Lambeth School of Art. Encouraged daily by Henry Doulton and given freedom to experiment, Hannah quickly developed her special talent while working on bird and foliage designs. By 1878, Hannah concentrated on portraying animals in a variety of settings: countryside, mountains, forest and jungle.

Hannah's forte was her ability to draw on paper and incise in damp clay the likeness of animals, using few strokes while capturing their natural movements. Her primary tech-

A sketch by Hannah Barlow for her own personalized Christmas cards, 1910.

nique involved the sgraffito (incised) method of decorating. She also painted Lambeth faience vases, tile panel plaques in low relief and the occasional pâte-sur-pâte piece.

Hannah's work in the early 1870s is simple and direct. During her most prolific period in the 1880s, she was capable of producing thirty different original pieces each week and was assisted by reigning artists Frank Butler, Emily Stormer, and Eliza Simmance, as well as her own sister, Florence.

Between 1881 and 1890, Hannah exhibited ten studies of animals modeled in high-relief terra cotta at the Royal Academy. She won numerous awards for her work at national and international exhibitions. Her distinguished art wares from a career spanning forty-two years remain a constant source of pleasure for collectors who appreciate wildlife scenes and simple design coupled with master technique.

Arthur (1871-1878)

Although Hannah's older brother Arthur joined the Lambeth Pottery with her in 1871, his artistic career was considerably shorter due to his untimely death. In 1869 Arthur followed Hannah to the Lambeth School of Art the year after she began her studies there. Even after their employment at Lambeth Pottery, both continued their studies at the Art School during the evenings.

Arthur Barlow concentrated on modeling where he practiced formalized decoration. He was known for working at a rapid speed, which enabled him to produce numerous mod-

Opposite page:
Original charcoal and pencil drawing of *Ye Fable of Ye Fox and Ye Crow* by Hannah Barlow

els with lavish foliage and scrolls in subdued colors. In spite of his poor health, Arthur was one of the most prolific artists at the pottery.

Like Hannah, Arthur was also given daily encouragement from Henry Doulton and both brother and sister developed their talents quickly. The International Exhibition of 1871 at the South Kensington Museum displayed and sold many Barlow creations.

When Arthur's health deteriorated to the point he could no longer attend work, he created drawings at home, which were then used by artists at the pottery to continue his unique designs. His early death in 1879 at the age of thirty-four created a challenging demand for Arthur Barlow pieces.

Florence (1873-1909)

Florence E. Barlow joined Arthur and Hannah at the Lambeth Pottery in 1873, a time when her style initially mimicked that of her sister. After several years, she found her specialty, notably pâte-sur-pâte painting, which became the most characteristic feature of her stoneware.

Initially, Hannah and Florence both incised animals and birds on their pots making their styles similar. Florence became prolific at drawing horses and other animals in a style similar to her sister's. Vases decorated by Florence can easily be confused with the work of Hannah. Florence developed a strong pattern sense long after Hannah had lost interest in formalized decoration. Hannah and Florence worked side-by-side much of the time-sharing a large studio where they frequently decorated vases and jugs together.

In the late 1870s, the sisters came to an informal agreement that Hannah would concentrate on animals while Florence would depict only birds. Soon Florence was known as "Birdie Barlow." The introduction of the pâte-sur-pâte tech-

MARKS.	DOVLTON WARE ARTISTS.	
⋀⋀⋀	Margaret Aitken	1
EA	Elizabeth Atkins	2
EⱭB	Eliza S. Banks	3
CSB	Clara S. Barker	4
ℋB	Hannah. B. Barlow	5
FEB	Florence E. Barlow	6
⅃Ⅾ	Louisa J. Davis	7
ꓠE	Louisa E. Edwards	8
Ⱶ	Elizabeth Fisher	9
ELH	Eliza L. Hubert	10
FEL	Frances E. Lee	11
EDL	Edith D. Lupton	12
MM	Mary Mitchell	13
FR	Florence C. Roberts	14

In 1882, the lady artists and assistants of the Lambeth studio, including Hannah and Florence Barlow, presented Henry Doulton with an illuminated manuscript containing each of their signatures.

nique allowed Florence to develop her own style. She was particularly successful in creating a sense of shadow on her pieces. In her later work, birds are sometimes drawn in a highly formalized Art Nouveau style.

Lucy (1882-1885)

After the rapid expansion of the Art Studio in the 1870s, the 1880s were a period of relative stability. The market for the salt-glazed and faience pieces had become saturated and new lines were introduced to stimulate the market. For a three-year period, from 1882-1885, another Barlow sister worked at the Art Studio. Lucy Barlow's decision to join Lambeth Pottery may have been associated with the illness and eventual death of their mother in 1882.

Lucy, older sister to Hannah and Florence, was employed as a decorator. Consequently, her work is most often associated with her younger sisters. Considered a minor talent, Lucy was responsible for executing borders and surrounding designs for Hannah and Florence. Lucy Barlow's association with the Art Studio ended by the mid-1880s and there is no mention of her in articles about the Barlows after 1886.

With her younger sisters both in their thirties and likely to remain spinsters, Lucy was invited to become their housekeeper. Hannah and Florence were established and happy in their pottery careers, and Lucy remained their housekeeper until their deaths. Today, the lucky collector may discover all three sisters' monograms incised on the bottom of a stoneware piece.

Original watercolor of a cow in the meadow by Hannah Barlow.

Pair of stoneware cups with incised mice and silver mounts, 1876. Hannah Barlow, artist. Doulton Lambeth backstamp, 5.25". (C)

Horse biscuit jar with silver lid and feet, 1874. Hannah Barlow, artist; Minnie Thompson, assistant. Doulton Lambeth backstamp, 6". (B)

Biscuit barrel with dogs, 1875. Hannah Barlow, artist; Maude Bowden, assistant. Doulton Lambeth backstamp, 5.5". (B)

Gesso vase with applied rosettes and beads, 1876. Hannah Barlow, artist; Mary Ann Thompson, assistant. Doulton Lambeth backstamp, 7.75". (B)

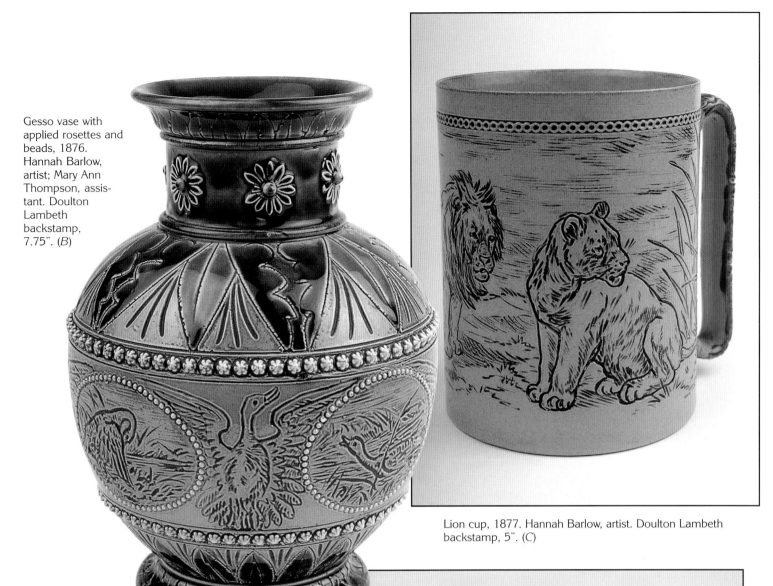

Lion cup, 1877. Hannah Barlow, artist. Doulton Lambeth backstamp, 5". (C)

Stoneware incised horse tyg, 1875. Hannah Barlow, artist; Ethel Beard, assistant. Doulton Lambeth backstamp, 6.5". (B)

Stoneware tyg with incised donkeys and silver engraved mount, 1878. Hannah Barlow, artist. Doulton Lambeth backstamp, 9.5". (B)

Lion pitcher with silver top, 1872. Hannah Barlow, artist; Minnie Thompson, assistant. Doulton Lambeth backstamp, 7.5". (C)

Multi-paneled lion vase with applied children medallions, 1877. Hannah Barlow and Frank A. Butler, artists; Mary Aitken, assistant. Doulton Lambeth backstamp, 26". (T)

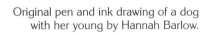

Original pen and ink drawing of a dog
with her young by Hannah Barlow.

Pair of horse vases,
1873. Hannah
Barlow, artist.
Doulton Lambeth
backstamp, 9". (C)

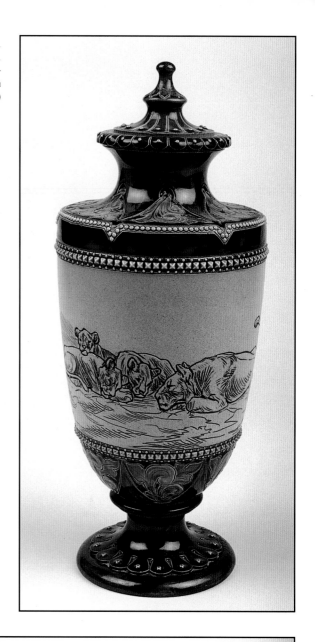

Lion and cub stoneware vase, c. 1880. Hannah Barlow, artist; Emily Stormer, assistant. Doulton Lambeth backstamp, 13". (*E*)

Lion vase with ornate handles, 1879. Hannah Barlow, artist; Rosina Brown and Francis E. Lee, assistants. Doulton Lambeth backstamp, 16.5". (*C*)

Pair of stoneware horse vases, c. 1880. Florence and Hannah Barlow, artists. Doulton Lambeth backstamp, 13". (*C*)

Pair of animal vases with elephant appliqués, 1876. Frank A. Butler and Hannah Barlow, artists. Doulton Lambeth backstamp, 13". (*D*)

Biscuit barrel incised with children playing with dogs and animals, 1879. Hannah Barlow, artist. Doulton Lambeth backstamp, 8.5". (*C*)

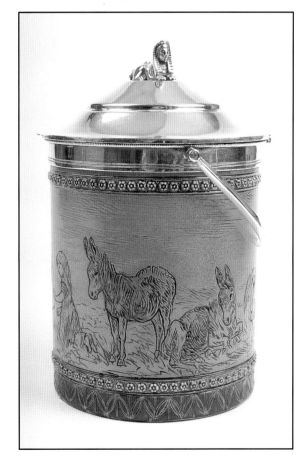

Teapot with chicken panels and dragon spout, snake handle and bird feet, 1879. Florence and Hannah Barlow, artists. Doulton Lambeth backstamp, 5". (C)

Fable of proud horse plaque, c. 1890. Hannah Barlow, artist. Doulton Lambeth backstamp, 9" x 9". (C)

Lion plaque, c. 1880. Hannah Barlow, artist. Doulton Lambeth backstamp, 9" x 9". (C)

Vase with children and animals, 1879. Hannah Barlow, artist; Louisa Wakely, assistant. Doulton Lambeth backstamp, 12.5". (C)

Pair of galloping horse vases, 1880. Hannah Barlow, artist. Doulton Lambeth backstamp, 10.5". (D)

Giraffes and lions among the trees, 1879. Hannah Barlow, artist; Clara S. Barker, assistant. Doulton Lambeth backstamp, 16.5". (L)

Lidded horse stoneware jar, 1884.
Florence and Hannah Barlow,
artists; Rosina Brown, assistant.
Doulton Lambeth backstamp,
6.25". (C)

Incised ploughing mug with rosettes on the rim, 1880. Hannah
Barlow, artist. Doulton Lambeth backstamp, 9.5". (C)

Stoneware ploughing vase,
c. 1880. Hannah Barlow, artist; Emma Burrows,
assistant. Doulton Lambeth backstamp, 10.5". (C)

Silver rimmed rabbit bowl, 1881. Hannah Barlow, artist. Doulton Lambeth backstamp, 5" x 9". (C)

Vase with horses, geese and a child, 1881. Hannah Barlow, artist; Mary Ann Thompson, assistant. Doulton Lambeth backstamp, 8.5". (C)

Inkwell with dogs and dog lid, 1880. Hannah Barlow, artist. Doulton Lambeth backstamp, 2.5". (C)

This page:
Noah's Arc lidded jar, 1881. Hannah Barlow, artist. Doulton Lambeth backstamp, 8". (*T*)

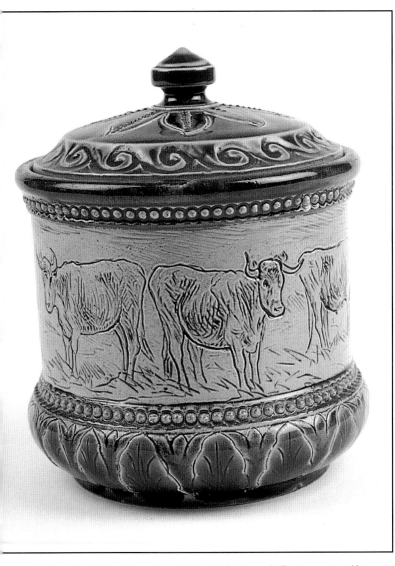

Incised bull biscuit barrel with lid, 1883. Hannah Barlow, artist; Kate Castle, assistant. Doulton Lambeth backstamp, 5". (B)

Pride of lions vase, 1884. Hannah Barlow, artist; Harriet Hibbut, assistant. Doulton Lambeth backstamp, 10.5". (C)

Pair of dog vases, 1883. Hannah and Lucy Barlow, artists; Emma A. Burrows, assistant. Doulton Lambeth backstamp, 8.25". (C)

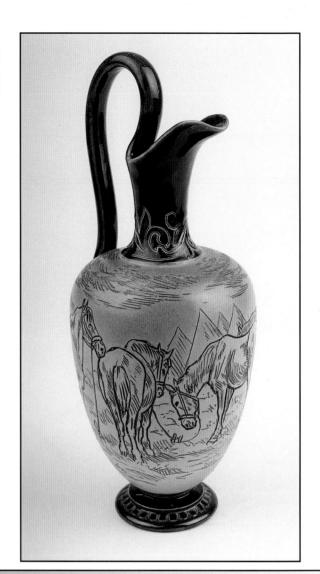

Pitcher with horses and tents in background, c. 1885. Hannah Barlow, artist. Doulton Lambeth backstamp, 10". (*C*)

Child and deer pitcher in patê-sur-patê, 1884. Hannah Barlow, artist. Doulton Lambeth backstamp, 9". (*B*)

Pair of vases with children and geese, 1884. Hannah Barlow, artist. Doulton Lambeth backstamp, 11.75". (*D*)

Biscuit barrel with lioness and cubs, 1883. Hannah Barlow, artist; Frank A. Butler and Annie Castle, assistants. Doulton Lambeth backstamp, 6.5". (*E*)

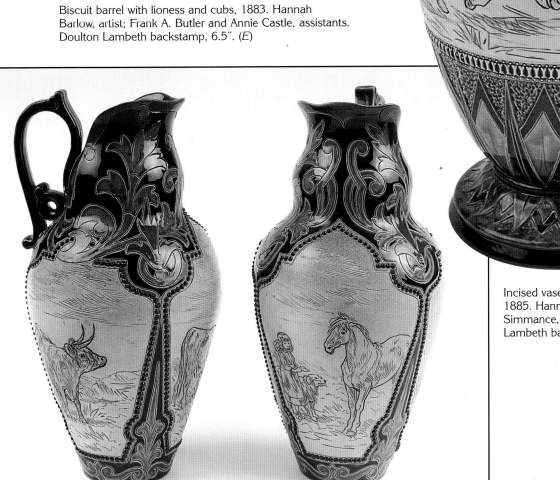

Incised vase with horses galloping, 1885. Hannah Barlow and Eliza Simmance, artists. Doulton Lambeth backstamp, 15". (*B*)

Pair of ewers with horse and bull panels, 1885. Hannah Barlow and Frank A. Butler, artists. Doulton Lambeth backstamp, 11.5". (*D*)

Faience moon flask with horses on front, donkey on back, c. 1880. Hannah Barlow, artist. Doulton Lambeth backstamp, 11'. (B)

Rabbit biscuit barrel with three panels in patê-sur-patê, 1884. Hannah and Lucy Barlow, artists. Doulton Lambeth backstamp, 6". (C)

Jardinière with horses in a field, 1883. Hannah Barlow, artist; Jenny Weekes, assistant. Doulton Lambeth backstamp, 9". (C)

Faience vase with horses, c. 1880. Hannah Barlow, artist. Doulton Lambeth backstamp, 17.5". (*B*)

Pitcher with incised horses and silver mount, 1886. Hannah Barlow, artist. Doulton Lambeth backstamp, 9.05". (*B*)

Oil on canvas of horse in pasture, c. 1890. Hannah Barlow, artist. 9". (*C*)

Pair of vases with incised white horses and trees in background, 1891. Hannah Barlow and Frank A. Butler, artists. Doulton Lambeth England backstamp, 28". (D)

Horse vase with long neck, c. 1891. Hannah Barlow, artist; Elizabeth J. Atkins, Jane Rumbol, assistants. Doulton Lambeth England backstamp, 16". (B)

Horse jardinière in panels with reticulated top and applied beads, c. 1890. Hannah Barlow and Frank A. Butler, artists; Rosina Brown, assistant. Doulton Lambeth backstamp, 10.5". (D)

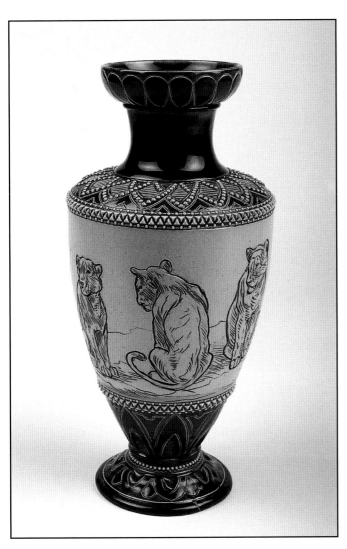

Lion vase, c. 1891. Hannah Barlow, artist. Doulton Lambeth England backstamp, 10.5". (D)

Pair of lion vases, c. 1891. Hannah Barlow, artist. Doulton Lambeth England backstamp, 8". (T)

Vase with lions and cubs, 1886. Hannah Barlow, artist. Doulton Lambeth backstamp, 11". (G)

Teapots, c. 1891. Hannah and Florence Barlow, artists; Elizabeth Fisher, assistant. Doulton Lambeth backstamp, 5". (*B*)

Dog tyg in patê-sur-patê, c. 1891. Hannah Barlow, artist; Florence Roberts, assistant. Doulton Lambeth England backstamp, 6.5". (*C*)

Horses incised on spittoon, 1890. Hannah Barlow, artist. Doulton Lambeth backstamp, 8". (*D*)

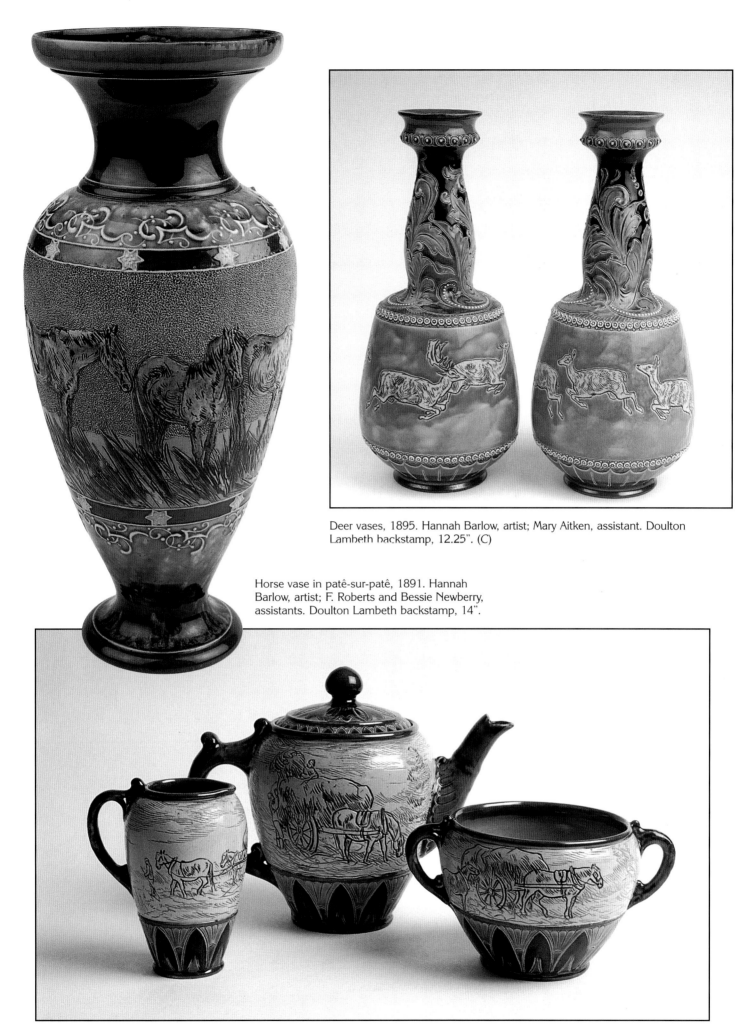

Deer vases, 1895. Hannah Barlow, artist; Mary Aitken, assistant. Doulton Lambeth backstamp, 12.25". (C)

Horse vase in patê-sur-patê, 1891. Hannah Barlow, artist; F. Roberts and Bessie Newberry, assistants. Doulton Lambeth backstamp, 14".

Farm scene stoneware tea set, c. 1892. Hannah Barlow, artist. Doulton Lambeth England backstamp, 6". (C)

Owl pitcher in patê-sur-patê with incised deer, c. 1891. Hannah and Florence Barlow, artists; Vera Huggins, assistant. Doulton Lambeth England backstamp, 12.5". (B)

Stoneware sheep spittoon, c. 1891. Florence and Hannah Barlow, artists; Vera Huggins, assistant. Doulton Lambeth England backstamp, 5.5". (B)

Vase with dogs on leash, c. 1891. Hannah Barlow, artist; Florence C. Roberts, assistant. Doulton Lambeth England backstamp, 9.5". (B)

Pair of multi-paneled vases with a child on a donkey, c. 1895. Hannah Barlow, artist; E. Fisher and R. Brown, assistants. Doulton Lambeth backstamp, 14.5". (*D*)

Pair of large three-handled vases with horse and cow panels, c. 1895. Hannah Barlow and Frank A. Butler, artists; Mary Aitken, assistant. Doulton Lambeth backstamp, 26". (*T*)

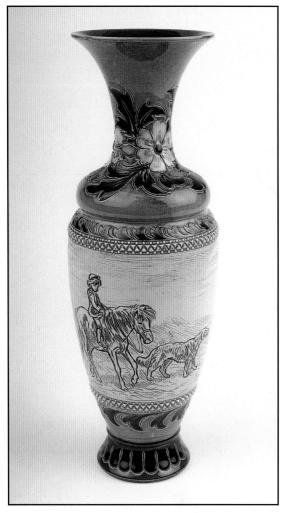

Child on a pony with dogs, 1895. Hannah Barlow, artist. Doulton Lambeth backstamp, 13". (C)

Cow vase in patê-sur-patê, c. 1891. Hannah Barlow, artist; Florence C. Roberts, assistant. Doulton Lambeth England backstamp, 18". (B)

Exhibition piece with horses and grotesque handle, c. 1895. Hannah and Florence Barlow, artists. Doulton Lambeth backstamp, 18.5". (T)

Arthur B. Barlow

Stoneware candlesticks, 1874. Arthur Barlow, artist.
Doulton Lambeth backstamp, 12". (*B*)

Jug with handle, foliate design
with silver mount, 1875. Arthur B.
Barlow, artist; Emma Martin,
assistant. 10". (*A*)

Pedestal dish with applied elephant handles and rosettes, 1875. Arthur B. Barlow, artist. Doulton Lambeth backstamp, 4". (*B*)

Fluted vase with angels in leaves, 1875. Arthur B. Barlow, artist. Doulton Lambeth backstamp, 8". (*B*)

Two-handled jug with foliate design, 1875. Arthur B. Barlow, artist. Doulton Lambeth backstamp, 7.25". (*A*)

Florence Barlow

Faience parakeet plaque, 1881. Florence Barlow, artist. Doulton Lambeth backstamp, 12" x 8". (B)

Paté-sur-paté turkey vase, c. 1885. Florence Barlow, artist; Florrie Jones, assistant. Doulton Lambeth backstamp, 10.75". (B)

Brown Peacock vase, 1883. Florence Barlow, artist; Mary Ann Thomson, assistant. Doulton Lambeth backstamp, 7.5". (*B*)

Duck vase in patê-sur-patê, c. 1891. Florence Barlow and Eliza Simmance, artists. Doulton Lambeth England backstamp, 12.5". (*B*)

Pair of bird vases, c. 1891. Florence Barlow, artist; Emma A. Burrows, assistant. Doulton Lambeth England backstamp, 16". (*C*)

Patê-sur-patê geese inkwell, c. 1885. Florence Barlow, artist; Bessie Newberry and A. Askew, assistants. Doulton Lambeth backstamp, 6". (C)

Patê-sur-patê pitcher with mermaid handle, c. 1891. Florence Barlow, artist; Francis E. Lee and Jane S. Hurst, assistants. Doulton Lambeth England backstamp, 15". (B)

Lambeth vase of bird and flowers in patê-sur-patê, 1895. Florence Barlow and Eliza Simmance, artists; Rosina Brown, assistant. 10.5". (B)

Pair of patê-sur-patê bird vases with applied faces, c. 1885. Florence Barlow and Frank A. Butler, artists. Doulton Lambeth backstamp, 13". (T)

Phoenix art nouveau stippled vase, 1895. Florence Barlow, artist. Doulton Lambeth backstamp, 16". (B)

Peacock vase with tube lining, c. 1895. Florence Barlow, artist. Doulton Lambeth backstamp, 12.5". (B)

Patê-sur-patê bird vase, 1895. Florence Barlow, artist. Doulton Lambeth backstamp, 14.5". (C)

Rooster vase in patê-sur-patê, c. 1895. Florence Barlow, artist; Emma Shute, assistant. Doulton Lambeth England backstamp, 10.75".

Mark V. Marshall (1880-1912)

One of Doulton's most talented modelers, Mark V. Marshall ex-celled in all aspects of pottery de-sign, but his grotesque sculptures of drag ons, lizards, and salamanders are most in teresting. Marshall worked in the Lambeth Studio from 1880 until his death in 1912 and examples of his architectural work can be found today on churches and hotels throughout England and Canada.

Mark Marshall was born in 1842 in Cranbrook, Kent, the son of a stonemason. Previously employed by the Martin Brothers, he began his career at Doulton on a freelance basis. Marshall had an extraordinary gift for incising and modeling wet clay, and he showed great spontaneity in his finely designed ornamental art wares. One of Marshall's most impressive pieces, an ewer standing over six feet high, was created for the Chicago Exhibition of 1893.

Taking leisurely walks through the streets of Kent, Marshall enjoyed the creatures he encountered,

which he then drew on his sketchpad. He was particularly partial to lizards and frequently used reptiles on the smaller pieces he modeled. The creatures snaked around the neck of a vase or battled with other animals.

While all types of animal and plant life inspired his work, he managed to include an element of humor in his interpretation of the world of nature. The faces of many of his creatures were caricatures of colleagues and people he met through his travels. Marshall often experimented with different techniques to discover what effect they would have in the clay.

He worked closely with the manager of the art department, Wilton Rix, in developing multi-colored, marbleized Mar-queterie wares. Marshall adorned the new range with his characteristic grotesque finials and handles. Inspired by the Art Nouveau movement, Marshall was adept at translating its feel into his pottery wares. Today, collectors who admire the work of Mark Marshall enjoy finding examples of his unique contribution to the Doulton line.

Figural candlestick of Adam and Eve under apple tree with serpent, a basket forming the candle sconce, 1878. Mark V. Marshall, artist. Doulton Lambeth backstamp, 16.25". (*E*)

Opposite page:
Mark V. Marshall working on his monumental ewer that was showcased at the Chicago Exhibition of 1893.

Lambeth vase with art nouveau sweeping leaves/flowers, 1878. Mark V. Marshall, artist. Doulton Lambeth backstamp, 15.5". (*B*)

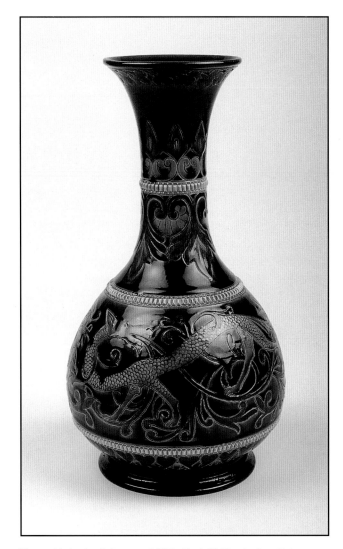

Vase with incised dragon, 1881. Mark V. Marshall, artist. Doulton Lambeth backstamp, 14". (*C*)

Pair of ewers with highly stylized features, 1887. Mark V. Marshall, artist; Emily Welch and Eliza Simmance, assistants. Doulton Lambeth backstamp, 10". (*D*)

Grotesque creature vase in dark blue, c. 1880. Mark V. Marshall, artist. Doulton Lambeth backstamp, 10.5". (*B*)

Pitcher with woman's head, 1880. Mark V. Marshall, artist; Rosina Brown, assistant. Doulton Lambeth backstamp, 9.5". (*B*)

Grotesque Wheatland terrier and serpent, 1885. Mark V. Marshall, artist. Doulton Lambeth backstamp, 11.25". (C)

Fish vase, 1880. Mark V. Marshall, artist. Doulton Lambeth backstamp, 7". (T)

Grotesque sculptured vase, c. 1880. Mark V. Marshall, artist. Doulton Lambeth backstamp, 22". (T)

Grotesque sculpted beast vase, 1885. Mark V. Marshall, artist. Doulton Lambeth backstamp, 10". (E)

Saltglazed art nouveau flower pitcher, c. 1895. Mark V. Marshall, artist; Bessie Newberry, assistant. Doulton Lambeth backstamp, 16". (*B*)

Lavishly modeled vase with scaly grotesque and its offspring, 1895. Mark V. Marshall, artist. Doulton Lambeth backstamp, 20". (*I*)

Three-fluted dragon vase, 1882. Mark V. Marshall, artist. Doulton Lambeth backstamp, 11". (*T*)

Vase with reticulated top and beaded detail, 1895. Mark V. Marshall, artist; Emily Clark, assistant. Doulton Lambeth backstamp, 10". (*C*)

Vase with base modeled as a rabbit's head, c. 1880. Mark V. Marshall, artist. Doulton Lambeth backstamp, 8.5". Exhibited at Los Angeles County Museum of Art, 1999, temporary loan. (C)

Group of animal studies, c. 1880. Mark V. Marshall, artist. Doulton Lambeth backstamp, 8". (B)

Pair of vases c. 1892. Left: green; right: blue. Mark V. Marshall, artist. Doulton Lambeth England backstamp, 11" & 10". (B)

Incised pitcher with attached red lid, c. 1895. Mark V. Marshall, artist. Doulton Lambeth backstamp, 10". (B)

Owl pitcher, c. 1891. Mark V. Marshall, artist; Bessie Newbury and Eleanor Tosen, assistants. Doulton Lambeth England backstamp, 10.5". (B)

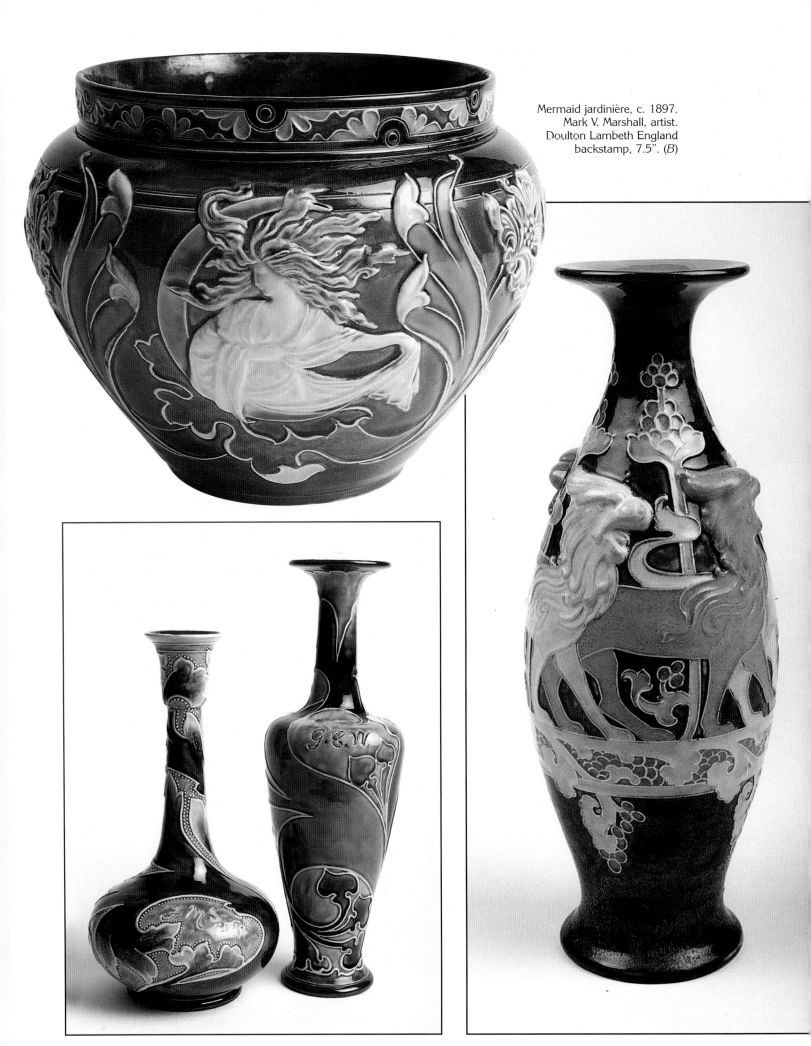

Mermaid jardinière, c. 1897.
Mark V. Marshall, artist.
Doulton Lambeth England
backstamp, 7.5". (B)

Pair of vases, personalized pieces made as gifts, c. 1892. Mark V. Marshall,
artist. Doulton Lambeth England backstamp, 10.5" & 12". (B)

Mystical creature vase, c. 1910. Mark V. Marshall, artist.
Royal Doulton England backstamp, 12.5". (C)

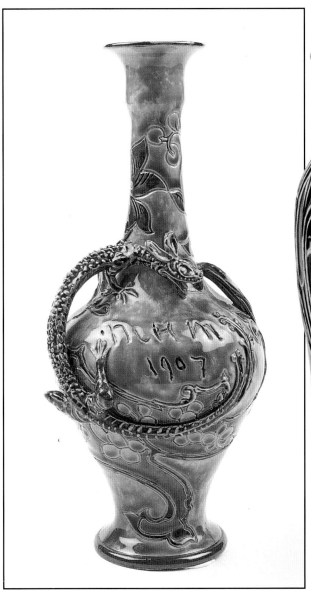

Two reptiles wrapped around a vase, 1907. Mark V. Marshall, artist; Bessie Newberry, assistant. Royal Doulton backstamp, 12". (B)

Open vase with scalloped owl heads around rim, c. 1895. Mark V. Marshall, artist. Doulton Lambeth backstamp, 8". (C)

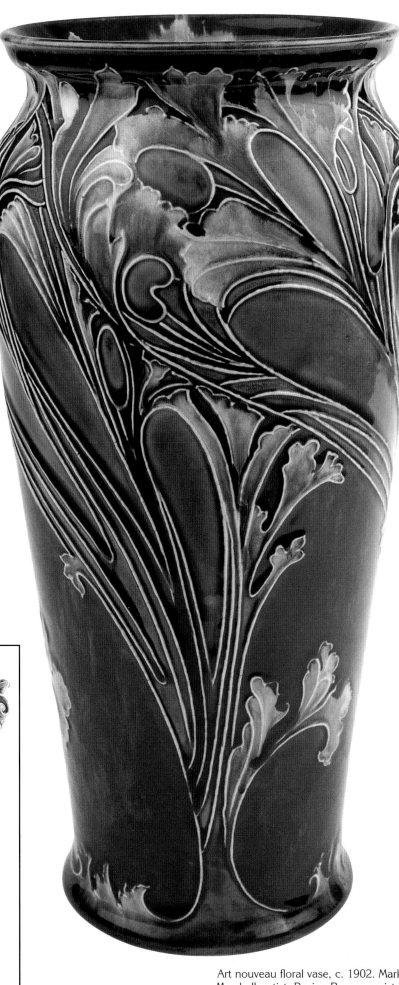

Art nouveau floral vase, c. 1902. Mark V. Marshall, artist; Rosina Brown, assistant. Doulton Lambeth backstamp, 13.5". (B)

89

Frank A. Butler (1872-1911)

One of the early Lambeth stoneware designers and decorators, Frank Butler worked for nearly forty years at his craft. He began his artistic career as a designer of stained glass but was soon introduced to ceramic arts by John Sparkes, Director of the Lambeth School of Art. This new medium allowed Butler to demonstrate both originality and invention.

Although he was both deaf and mute, Butler was a versatile artist who became one of the best-known personalities in the art world. The public enjoyed observing Frank at Doulton exhibitions as he created and decorated vases, jugs, bowls, and pots on stage. His early work was geometric and repetitive massing together floral forms with discs, dots, and intertwining lines. Frank's talent was especially evident when he pressed, folded, and snapped wet clay into shapes other than circular. He reveled in the plasticity of the clay.

Queen Victoria and her Prime Minister Gladstone expressed their admiration for Frank Butler's work. His Indian Pavilion was selected by Doulton as one of the centerpieces for the Glasgow Exhibition of 1888. Having the ability to adapt to changing tastes and styles enabled Butler to work well in the fluid lines of the Art Nouveau fashion. His design inspiration radically changed the Doulton production, resulting in some of the most extravagant pieces produced at the Lambeth Studio. Although the peak of his artistic career occurred in the 1890s, Butler was responsible for the creation of thousands of decorative wares over his forty-year reign at Doulton.

Trio of Doulton Lambeth stoneware vases. Left to right: boldly tube-lined with stylized water lilies, c. 1890. 10.25". (C); tube-lined and molded with upright stylized plant stems, 1901. 15". (D); molded in low relief with stylized peacock feathers, c. 1890. Doulton Lambeth backstamp, 10.25". (D). Frank A. Butler, artist.

Opposite page:
Frank A. Butler, c.1905, working in his studio on a stoneware centerpiece.

Pitcher with Pegasus handle, 1879. Frank A. Butler, artist. Doulton Lambeth backstamp, 10". (B)

Cherubs on jardinière, 1877. Frank A. Butler, artist. Doulton Lambeth backstamp, 5.25". (B)

Jardinière with children figures in flowers, 1882. Frank Butler, artist; H. Hibbut & E. Burrell, assistants. Doulton Lambeth backstamp, 8". (*B*)

Vase with small cameo, 1881. Frank A. Butler, artist; Isabella Miller, Emma Burrows and Rosetta Hazeldine, assistants. Doulton Lambeth backstamp, 6.75". (A)

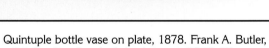

Quintuple bottle vase on plate, 1878. Frank A. Butler, artist. Doulton Lambeth backstamp, 10.5". (A)

Stoneware vase incised with twisted stylized foliage below a pierced and carved neck, c. 1880. Frank A. Butler, artist; John Huskinson, assistant. Doulton Lambeth backstamp, 15.5".

Flower vase with inscribed leaves and applied flower heads, 1882. Frank A. Butler, artist; Dunn and Hubert, assistants. Doulton Lambeth backstamp. 10.5". (B)

Bottleneck vase
with dragon
appliqués,
c. 1880. Frank A.
Butler, artist; Mary
Aitken, assistant.
Doulton Lambeth
backstamp, 9.5".
(A)

Pitcher with poppy heads,
1885. Frank A. Butler,
artist. Doulton Lambeth
backstamp, 11". (C)

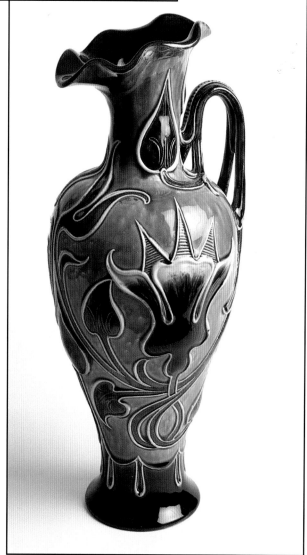

Lambeth blue and
brown sculpted ewer,
1887. Frank A. Butler,
artist. 6.25". (B)

Vase with handle and swirled edge, c. 1891.
Frank A. Butler, artist; Bessie Newberry, assistant. Doulton Lambeth England, 19". (C)

Vase with leaves and squished form, 1885. Frank A. Butler, artist. Doulton Lambeth backstamp, 10". (C)

Vase with curved lipped edge, c. 1892. Frank A. Butler, artist; Emily Partington, assistant. Doulton Lambeth England backstamp, 13.5". (B)

Lambeth paisley vase, 1895. Frank A. Butler, artist; Hurst and Rumbel, assistants. Doulton Lambeth backstamp, 11" (B)

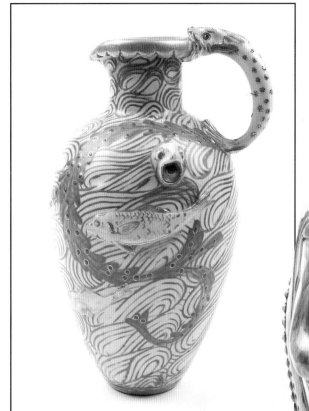

Carrera ware pitcher with relief fish on body and fish handle, c. 1895. Frank A. Butler, artist. Doulton Lambeth backstamp, 9.5". (C)

Ginkgo leaf vase, c. 1900. Frank A. Butler, artist; Bessie Newberry, assistant. Doulton Lambeth backstamp, 14". (C)

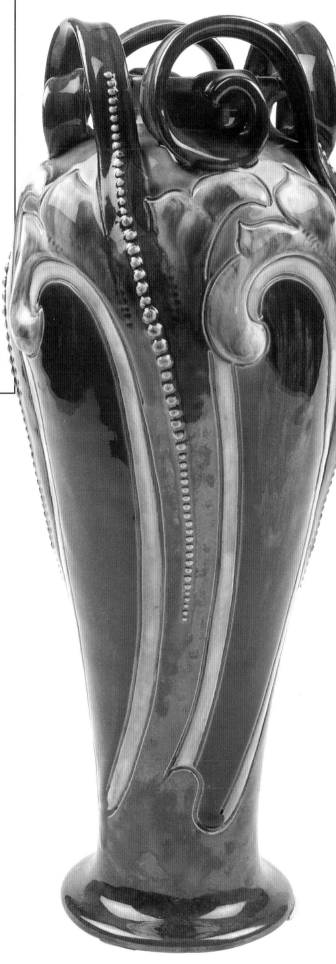

Royal Doulton Lambeth stoneware vase with highly stylized foliage extending to four applied spiral strap handles, 1903. Frank A. Butler, artist. Doulton Lambeth backstamp, 14.5". (B)

Other Lambeth Artists

Stoneware bowl with owl feet, 1881. Ella Adams, artist. Doulton Lambeth backstamp, 5". (*B*)

Candlestick with foliate design, 1877. Margaret Aitken, artist; Annie Gentle, assistant. Doulton Lambeth backstamp, 5.25". (*B*)

Monkey bookends, c. 1880. William Leonard Baron, artist. Doulton Lambeth England backstamp, 7". (*B*)

Stoneware fish vase, 1883. William Baron, artist; Rosina Brown, assistant. Doulton Lambeth backstamp, 8". (*A*)

Vase with reticulated appliqués, 1879. Mary Capes, artist. Doulton Lambeth backstamp, 10.5". (*C*)

John Broad

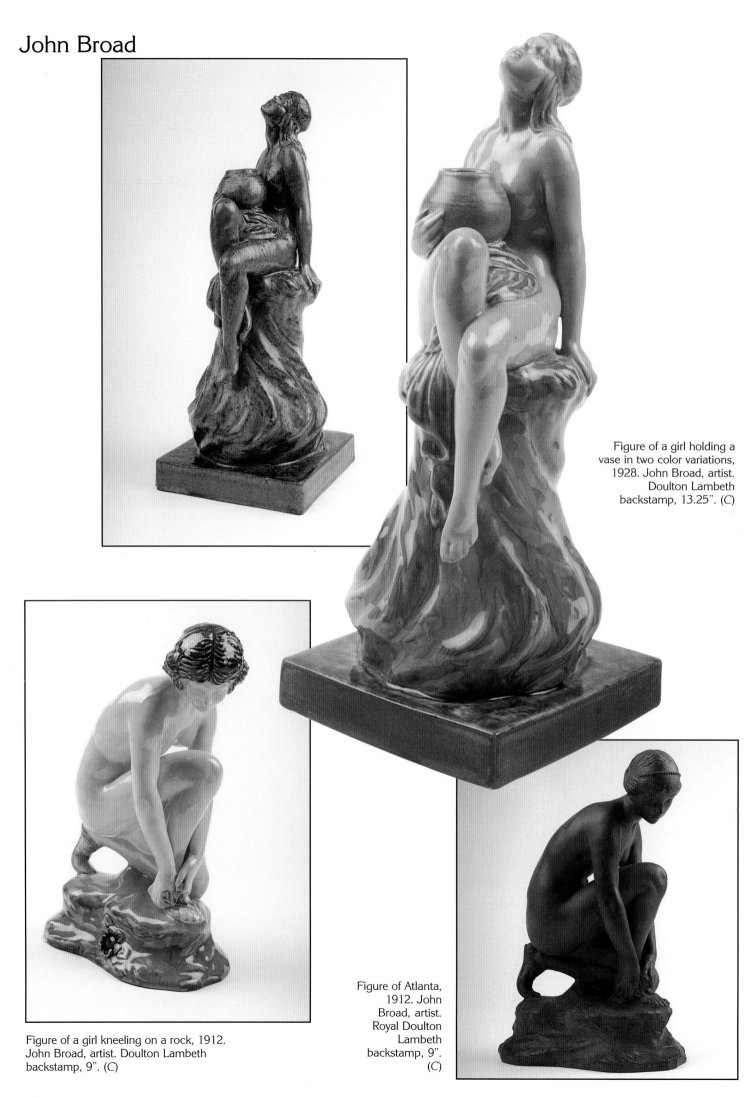

Figure of a girl holding a vase in two color variations, 1928. John Broad, artist. Doulton Lambeth backstamp, 13.25". (C)

Figure of a girl kneeling on a rock, 1912. John Broad, artist. Doulton Lambeth backstamp, 9". (C)

Figure of Atlanta, 1912. John Broad, artist. Royal Doulton Lambeth backstamp, 9". (C)

Figure of a bather, 1912. John Broad, artist. Doulton Lambeth backstamp, 12". (*D*)

Figure of a bather, 1912. John Broad, artist. Doulton Lambeth backstamp, 13". (*B*)

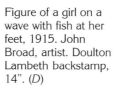

Figure of a bather in a color variation, c. 1912. John Broad, artist. Doulton Lambeth backstamp, 14". (*B*)

Figure of a girl on a wave with fish at her feet, 1915. John Broad, artist. Doulton Lambeth backstamp, 14". (*D*)

"This Little Pig" child study variation one and two, c. 1912. Leslie Harradine, artist. Royal Doulton backstamp, 5" & 4.5". (A)

Figure of a monkey, c. 1912. Leslie Harradine, artist. Doulton Lambeth England backstamp, 8". (B)

"Votes for Women" inkwells-2 variations, 1905. Leslie Harradine, artist. Royal Doulton backstamp, 3.5". (A)

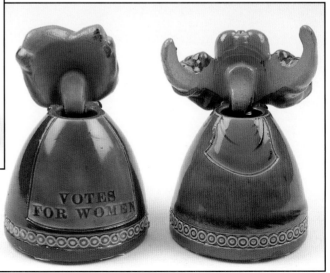

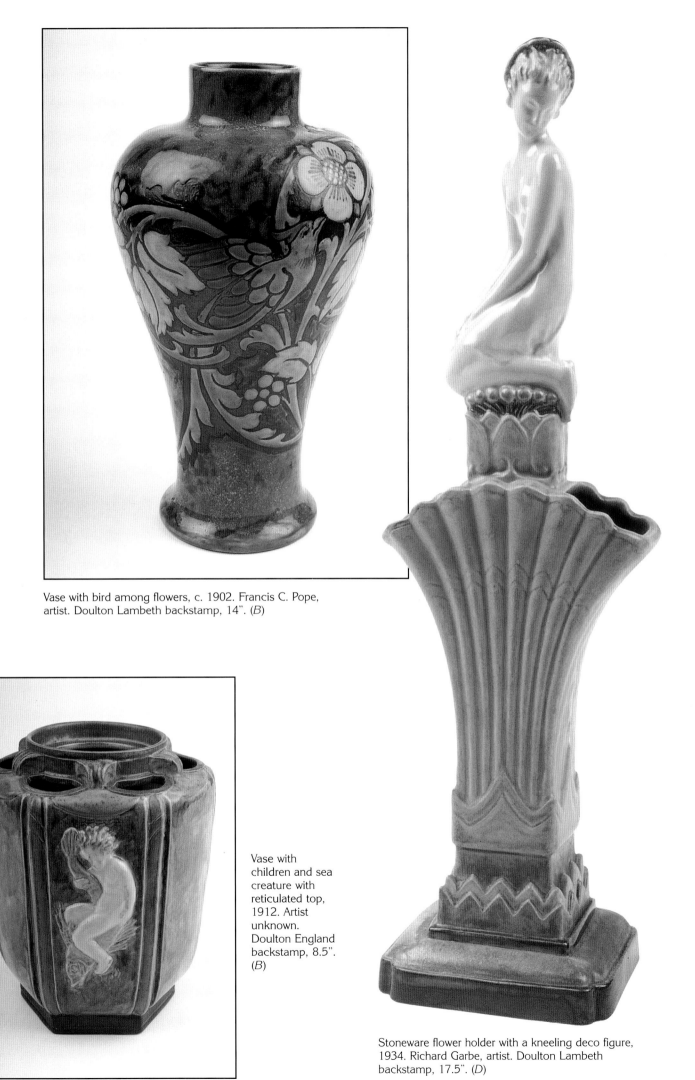

Vase with bird among flowers, c. 1902. Francis C. Pope, artist. Doulton Lambeth backstamp, 14". (B)

Vase with children and sea creature with reticulated top, 1912. Artist unknown. Doulton England backstamp, 8.5". (B)

Stoneware flower holder with a kneeling deco figure, 1934. Richard Garbe, artist. Doulton Lambeth backstamp, 17.5". (D)

Stoneware pitcher with peacock on handle, 1885. Edith Lupton, artist; Jane Hurst, assistant. Doulton Lambeth backstamp, 9". (A)

Narrow pitcher with beach scene, 1890. Edith D. Lupton, artist. Doulton Lambeth backstamp, 8". (B)

Three-legged bowl with poppies and modeled owl feet, 1881. Louisa J. Davis, artist; Harriet Hibbut, assistant. Doulton Lambeth backstamp, 5". (B)

Mantle clock with incised floral sides and finial corners, 1884. Frances E. Lee, artist; Maud Bowden, assistant. Doulton Lambeth backstamp, 13". (D)

Footed mantle clock with foliate design, 1879. Frances E. Lee, artist. Doulton Lambeth backstamp, 10.5". (C)

Three female busts wearing Egyptian style peacock headdresses, 1886. Eliza L. Hubert and John Huskinson, artists; Mary Ann Thompson, assistant. Doulton Lambeth backstamp, 29". (*l*)

Stoneware desk tray with reticulated sides with gargoyles, 1878. Mary Ann Thompson, artist; Eleanor Burrell, assistant. Doulton Lambeth backstamp, 10" x 2.5". (B)

Ornate wall pocket, c. 1890. Artist unknown. Doulton Lambeth backstamp, 12.5" x 17". (A)

Mary Mitchell

Pair of child candlesticks, 1880. Mary Mitchell, artist; Mary Ann Thompson, assistant. Doulton Lambeth backstamp, 10.25". (C)

People at seaside with flowers on top of vase, 1880. Mary Mitchell, artist; Mary Aitken, assistant. Doulton Lambeth backstamp, 10". (B)

Vase of girls playing a game, 1881. Mary Mitchell, artist. Doulton Lambeth backstamp, 10.75". (B)

Pair of incised vases with people on panels and flowers incised on top, 1881. Mary Mitchell, artist; Mary Aitken, assistant. Doulton Lambeth backstamp, 9.5". (C)

Covered stein of boy and girl, c. 1880. Mary Mitchell, artist. Doulton Lambeth backstamp, 9". (B)

Pied Piper figure, 1915. G.H. Pahlin, artist. Doulton Lambeth backstamp, 12". (*D*)

Vase with dragon wrapped around flowers, 1879. Artist unknown. Doulton Lambeth backstamp, 10.75". (*A*)

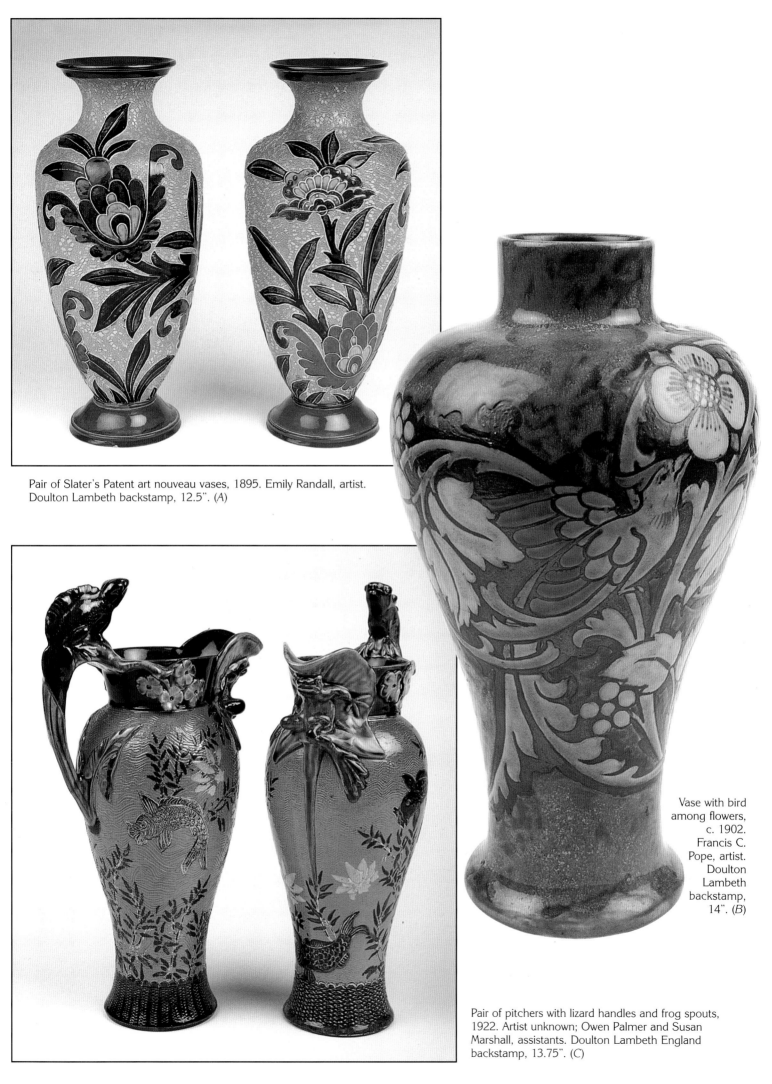

Pair of Slater's Patent art nouveau vases, 1895. Emily Randall, artist. Doulton Lambeth backstamp, 12.5". (A)

Vase with bird among flowers, c. 1902. Francis C. Pope, artist. Doulton Lambeth backstamp, 14". (B)

Pair of pitchers with lizard handles and frog spouts, 1922. Artist unknown; Owen Palmer and Susan Marshall, assistants. Doulton Lambeth England backstamp, 13.75". (C)

Pair of modeled goshawk with oak leaves and acorns,
c. 1885. William Parker, artist; Annie Gentle, assistant.
Doulton Lambeth backstamp, 19". (*T*)

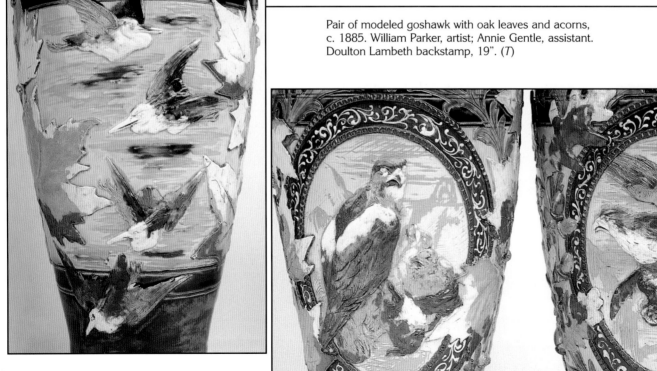

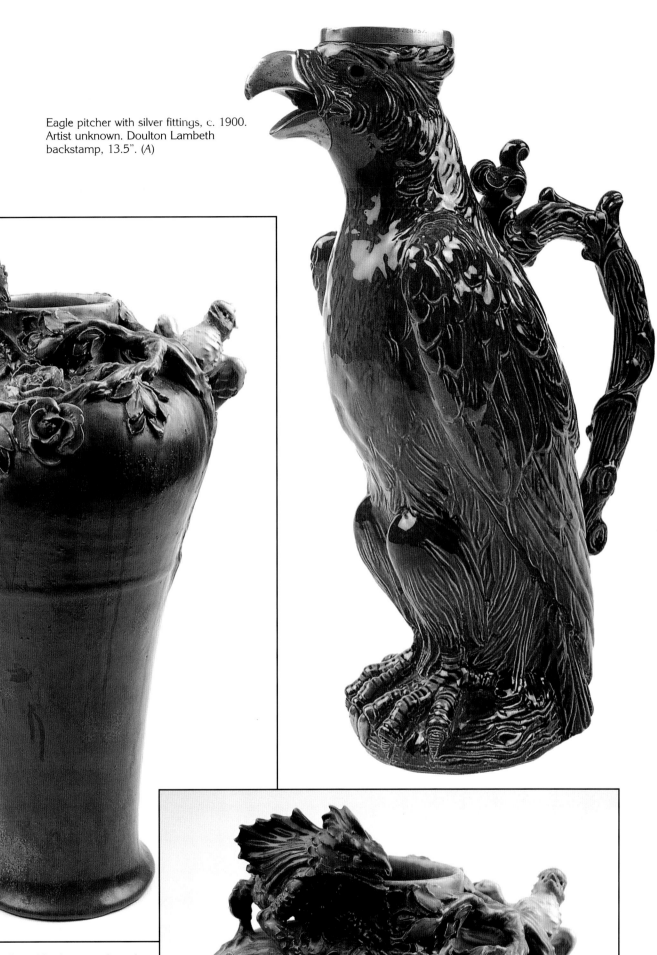

Eagle pitcher with silver fittings, c. 1900.
Artist unknown. Doulton Lambeth
backstamp, 13.5". (A)

Vase with reptile and bird on rose branch,
c. 1910. Francis C. Pope, artist; J.H. Sale,
assistant. Doulton England backstamp, 18". (D)

Eliza Simmance

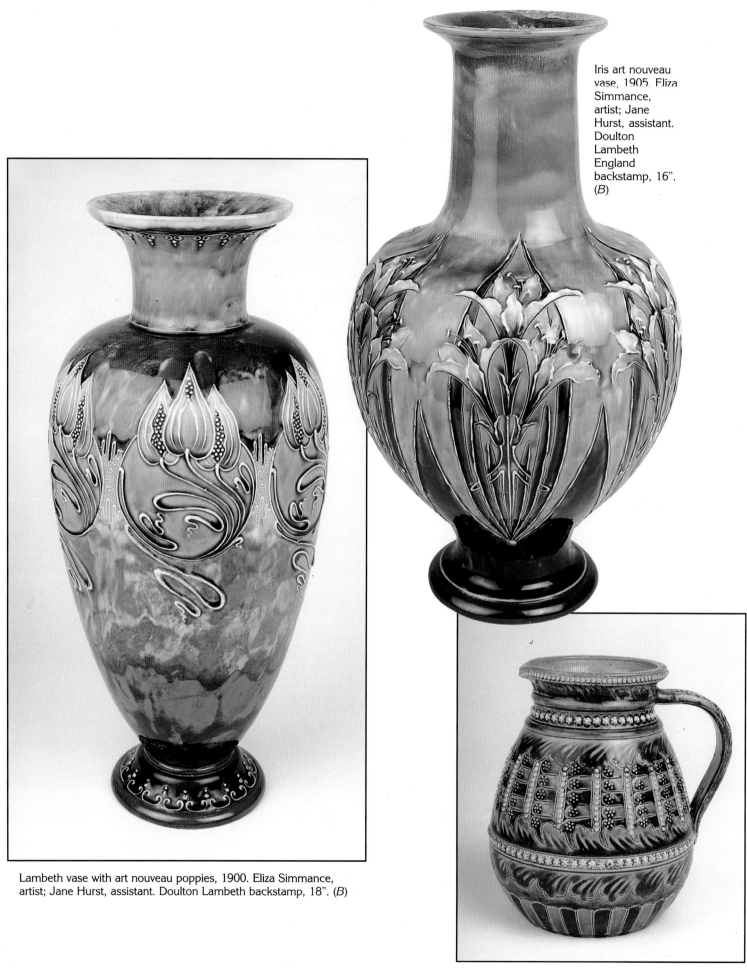

Iris art nouveau vase, 1905. Eliza Simmance, artist; Jane Hurst, assistant. Doulton Lambeth England backstamp, 16". (B)

Lambeth vase with art nouveau poppies, 1900. Eliza Simmance, artist; Jane Hurst, assistant. Doulton Lambeth backstamp, 18". (B)

Incised and applied pitcher with lavender slip, 1875. Eliza Simmance, artist; Emma Martin, assistant. Doulton Lambeth backstamp, 6.5". (A)

Pair of art nouveau peacock feathered vases, 1910. Eliza Simmance, artist. Doulton Lambeth backstamp, 9". (*B*)

Pair of vases with light blue accent, c. 1897. Eliza Simmance, artist; Rosina Brown, assistant. Doulton Lambeth England backstamp, 14". (*B*)

Sea horse vase with applied beads, 1906. Eliza Simmance, artist. Doulton Lambeth England backstamp, 14". (*B*)

Vase with applied beads and florets, 1886. Eliza Simmance, artist. Doulton Lambeth backstamp, 19". (*C*)

Art nouveau vase for Art Union of London, c. 1895. Eliza Simmance, artist. Doulton Lambeth backstamp, 16". (*B*)

Pair of stoneware vases. Left: Globular vase, c. 1892. Eliza Simmance, artist; Bessie Newbury, assistant. Doulton Lambeth England backstamp, 14.5". (B) Right: Double-handled vase, 1877. Emily E. Stormer, artist; Mary Aitken, assistant. Doulton Lambeth backstamp, 15". (B)

Cameo vase with blue glaze and brown relief, 1902. Artist unknown. Doulton Lambeth backstamp, 12". (B)

Pair of stoneware lady figurehead wall mounts, 1876. Artist unknown. Attributed to Doulton Lambeth. 10". (C)

Brown stoneware pitcher with ornate lip and handle, c. 1891. Bessie Newberry, artist. Doulton Lambeth England backstamp, 11.5". (B)

Pair of fresco panels of Botticelli's
"Primavera," c. 1890. William Rowe,
artist. Doulton Lambeth backstamp,
12" x 9". (*T*)

119

Mini flower vase, c. 1878.
Harry Simeon, artist;
Bessie Newberry, assis-
tant. Doulton Lambeth
backstamp, 5". (A)

Humidifier for conservatory, 1885. Pearce, Roberts
and Partington, artists. Doulton Lambeth
backstamp, 13". (B)

Four variations of the "baby" inkwell, c. 1905. Harry Simeon,
artist. Doulton Lambeth backstamp, 3.75". (A)

Grotesque figure thinking, c. 1900. Artist unknown. Doulton Lambeth backstamp, 4". (*B*)

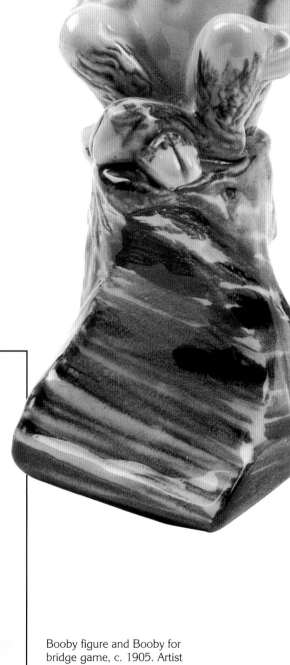

Pan on stoneware base, c. 1925. Artist unknown. Royal Doulton backstamp, 5.5". (*B*)

Booby figure and Booby for bridge game, c. 1905. Artist unknown. Doulton Lambeth backstamp, 4". (*B*)

Doulton Lambeth stoneware vase with dragon and wings wrapped around body, 1881. Harry Barnard, artist. Doulton Lambeth backstamp, 15". (D)

Gryphons candlestick, c. 1880. Harriet Hibbert, artist; Isabella Miller, assistant. Doulton Lambeth backstamp, 8". (B)

Incised dish with sterling flower bud lid and tray, 1881. Minnie Thompson, artist. Doulton Lambeth backstamp, 4". (A)

Incised foliate inkwell with leafed pattern, 1878. Artist unknown. Doulton Lambeth backstamp, 4.5". (A)

Polar bear with young,
1927. Artist unknown.
Doulton Lambeth
backstamp, 11". (B)

Creature with brush back, 1900. Artist unknown.
Doulton Lambeth backstamp, 1.5". (A)

Jar with monkey lid, glass eyes and silver pipe, 1910.
Artist unknown. Royal Doulton backstamp, 6". (A)

Doulton Faience (1873-1914)

Doulton Faience – colorful and vibrant in its decorative effect – was mistakenly one of the most underrated products of the highly successful Lambeth Studio. In 1872, one year after the Doulton Company's first successful exhibition, Henry Doulton and John Sparkes eagerly launched innovative art ceramics when they created the Faience studio. Great improvements in ceramic production as well as the refinement of designs and colors became the hallmark of their new art studio at Lambeth.

Experimenting for a year in an attempt to reproduce the admired features of hand-painted Majolica ware, the artists introduced the first Doulton Faience pieces in 1873. This new earthenware was finer and paler than its stoneware predecessor, allowing more subtle decorative treatments and a wider palette of colors. Meticulous attention was imperative during the firing process to ensure that the colors and glazes would expand and contract in perfect harmony, thus avoiding hairline cracks.

The technique of painting and decorating in this new medium proved demanding for the studio's expanding group of art students. New colors, derived mainly from metallic oxides, were painted directly onto the porous, unglazed earthenware body.

Any mistake could be easily detected because of the rapid manner in which the color soaked into the clay. In addition, many of the colors used underwent changes when the biscuit form was fired, forcing the skilled artists to visualize the completed piece before it emerged from the kiln. After the colors were applied, a second firing called "hardening-on" set the colors before the piece was glazed. After its third firing, a piece could be decorated with additional over-glaze enameled coloring or gilding, which would require yet a fourth firing. This over-glaze firing allowed a much broader palette than could be obtained by using only under-glaze colors.

This exciting style of painting was used on different types of decorative and domestic wares, including vases, wall plaques, biscuit barrels, and teapots. The most popular decorations included floral designs in both natural and Art Nouveau styles. Faience ceramic tiles were also produced depicting views of London, landscapes, and Shakespearean subjects, as well as popular nursery rhymes. Elaborate tile panels of Doulton Faience adorned the children's wards of respected hospitals of the period. Other subjects included figure studies, portraits, and birds painted onto a wide range of shapes and sizes.

Doulton faience tile of Little Red Riding Hood in her Grandmother's Cottage. This panel was designed for a children's ward at a New Zealand hospital.

Opposite page:
Doulton Lambeth showroom highlighting Doulton Faience vases and plaques, c. 1895.

At the Philadelphia Exhibition of 1876, Doulton unveiled Faience to an enthusiastic public. Even the beloved Queen Victoria was impressed by the Faience wares and promoted Doulton's latest success around Europe. In 1878, at the Paris Exhibition, Faience pieces were once again displayed and critically acclaimed.

Artists at the new studio began specializing in Faience. The Barlow sisters, Hannah and Florence, along with Eliza Simmance, who had all gained earlier recognition at Lambeth, occasionally lent their talents to the Faience studio producing magnificent pieces of work on plaques and moon-shaped vases. Three of the most notable artists to emerge from the Faience studio were Florence (1874-1897) and Esther Lewis (1877-1897) and Linnie Watt (1874-1890). Esther Lewis specialized in woodland scenes and seascapes while Watt focused on figure painting and landscapes. Florence Lewis, a skilled painter of flowers, foliage and birds, produced Doulton's most impressive recorded piece of Faience for the Chicago Exhibition of 1893. Her creation stood over six feet high and three feet in diameter.

Senior artists were allowed to concentrate their talent and energy on the more demanding tasks of design and decoration, while assistant artists were employed to paint backgrounds or less difficult parts of the design. Senior artist John McLennan (1880-1910) produced impressive tiles and murals in an Art Nouveau style while the versatile artist, John Eyre (1883-1897), excelled in figure studies, landscapes, and mythological designs. Mary Capes (1876-1885), another accomplished senior artist, drew her inspiration from Japanese art and design as she developed her own painting technique.

Faience pieces appeared in a variety of designs, subject matter and colors as well as a diverse array of shapes and sizes. In 1910 the production of Faience started to dwindle. The last recorded wares are dated 1914. Made for a relatively short period, Faience pieces in good condition prove difficult to find and provide an exciting challenge for the collector.

The "Earth Goddess" faience tile panel supplied by Doulton to John Shorter and Company, a retailer in Sydney, Australia. There were four panels displayed at Shorter and Company at the turn of the 20th century, but this is the only panel to survive when the building was demolished in 1937.

126

Doulton faience tile panel of Mary, Mary Quite Contrary by Margaret E. Thompson, c. 1900.

Artists painting and decorating art wares in the Lambeth Faience studio, c. 1890.

Faience vase with flowers in amber and teal, 1880. Mary A. Arding, artist. Doulton Lambeth backstamp, 23.5". (B)

Pair of faience vases with irises, c. 1880. Helen Arding, artist. Doulton Lambeth backstamp, 12.5". (C)

Faience vase with fall leaves of red, yellow, green, and brown, c. 1880. Alice Marshall, artist. Doulton Lambeth backstamp, 13". (A)

Pair of faience vases with little girls on each, c. 1880. Margaret M. Armstrong, artist. Doulton Lambeth backstamp, 9.5". (B)

The "Fairies at the Christening" faience tile panel by Margaret Thompson, c. 1908. The panel was designed for Manchester's Children's Hospital.

Pair of vases with children, reticulated top and center, c. 1900. Ada Dennis, artist; J. Durtnall, assistant. Doulton Lambeth backstamp, 12". (C)

Fruit and flower double handled faience vase, 1878. Mary Capes, artist. Doulton Lambeth backstamp, 15". (C)

Decorated faience vase with cherubs, 1892. Mary Denley, artist; Josephine Durtnall, assistant. Doulton Lambeth backstamp, 17.5". (T)

A print of a drawing dated 1893, designed by W. Rowe for one of several tile panels shown at the Chicago Exhibition of 1893. The drawing depicts artists working on faience pieces.

Trio of Doulton Faience vases, c. 1880. Artist for tall vase: Ada Dennis; medium vase: Mary Denley & Esther Lewis; small vase: Urlizue Larcher. Doulton Faience backstamp, 4", 9", 12". (B)

Faience vase of women and two children, c. 1880. Ada Dennis, artist. Doulton Lambeth backstamp, 10". (B)

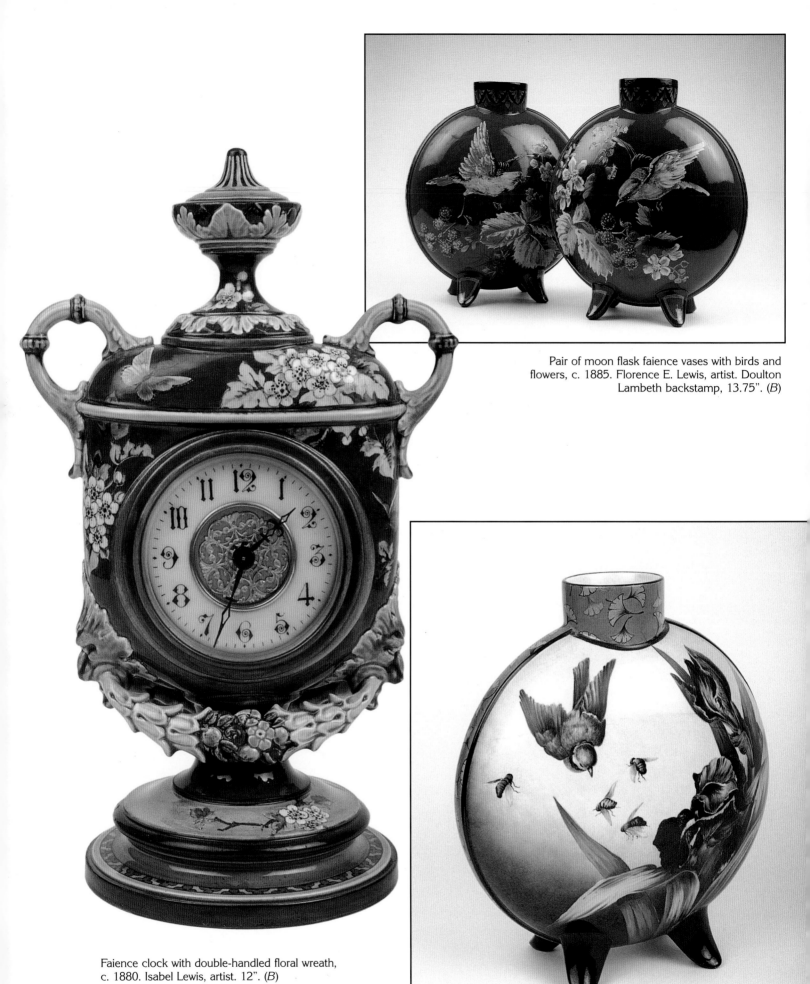

Pair of moon flask faience vases with birds and flowers, c. 1885. Florence E. Lewis, artist. Doulton Lambeth backstamp, 13.75". (*B*)

Faience clock with double-handled floral wreath, c. 1880. Isabel Lewis, artist. 12". (*B*)

Pilgrim faience moon flask with blue tit and insects, c. 1890. Mary Butterton and Alice Campbell, artists. Doulton Lambeth backstamp, 14.25". (*B*)

John H. McLennan

Pair of faience vases with cherubs, 1890. John H. McLennan, artist. Doulton Lambeth backstamp, 23". (C)

John H. McLennan painting a faience vase in his studio, c. 1900.

Faience female figure in billowing dress, c. 1890. John H. McLennan, artist. Doulton Lambeth backstamp, 22". (D)

Faience pomegranate vase, 1907. Eliza Simmance, artist; Bessie Newberry, assistant. Doulton Lambeth England backstamp, 15.5". (*B*)

Pair of flowers and tendrils art nouveau faience vases, 1906. Eliza Simance, artist; Florrie Jones, assistant. Doulton Lambeth England backstamp, 14". (*B*)

Windswept vase, c. 1900. John H. McLennen, artist. Doulton Lambeth backstamp, 12.5". (*C*)

Man feeding woman in faience, c. 1890. Walter J. Nunn, artist. Doulton Lambeth backstamp, 11.25". (*B*)

A.E. Thatcher

Lambeth faience large mantel clock case, c. 1880. A.E. Thatcher, artist. Doulton Lambeth backstamp, 15.5". (B)

Faience clock with apple blossoms and elephant handles, c. 1880. A.E. Thatcher, artist; B.L. Robinson, assistant. Doulton Lambeth backstamp, 10". (B)

Faience vase with angels, c. 1910. Margaret E. Thompson, artist. Doulton Lambeth backstamp, 14.5". (*C*)

Faience vase of two mermaids amongst a school of fish and elongated seaweed, 1890. Margaret E. Thompson, artist. Doulton Lambeth backstamp, 13.25". (*F*)

Faience vase with slim neck, 1876. Artist unknown. Doulton Lambeth backstamp, 15". (*B*)

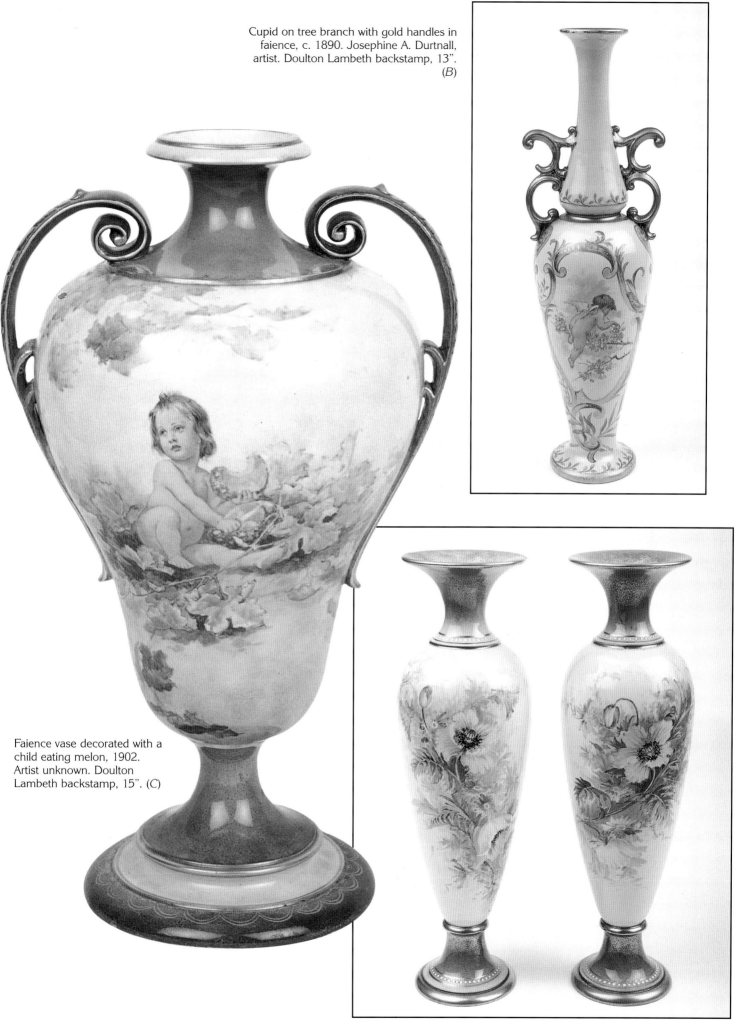

Cupid on tree branch with gold handles in faience, c. 1890. Josephine A. Durtnall, artist. Doulton Lambeth backstamp, 13". (B)

Faience vase decorated with a child eating melon, 1902. Artist unknown. Doulton Lambeth backstamp, 15". (C)

Faience pair of floral vases, 1876. Artist unknown. Doulton Lambeth backstamp, 11.5". (B)

Linnie Watt

Faience plaque of
children in field at
harvest, c. 1890. L. Watt,
artist. Doulton Lambeth
backstamp, 12". (B)

In 1885, "The Leisure Hour" publication ran this drawing of artists working in the
Lambeth studio.

Faience plaque of woman at lake in contemplation, c. 1880.
L. Watt, artist. Doulton Lambeth backstamp, 8.25". (B)

Faience plaque of woman on bridge, c. 1890. L. Watt, artist. Doulton Lambeth backstamp, 14" x 8" oval. (B)

Plaque of woman admiring swan, c. 1900. L. Watt, artist. Doulton Lambeth backstamp, 14" x 8" oval. (C)

Faience plaque
of woman with
blue hat, c. 1890.
James R. Cruickshank,
artist. Doulton Lambeth
backstamp, 18". (C)

Faience plaque of girl with bonnet, c. 1880. Artist
unknown. Doulton Lambeth backstamp, 13". (B)

Faience plaque of woman's face with veil on head, c. 1880.
Artist unknown. Doulton Lambeth backstamp, 15.5". (C)

Faience plaque of children on snowy pond, 1875. Artist unknown. Doulton Lambeth backstamp, 12.5". (*B*)

Faience hand-painted tile entitled "Fire," c. 1900. Artist unknown. Doulton Lambeth backstamp, 9" x 9". (*B*)

Faience plaque of "Midsummer Night's Dream," c. 1890. Artist unknown. Doulton Lambeth backstamp, 12" x 8". (*C*)

Faience plaque of two women sitting, 1890. L. Welt, artist. Doulton Lambeth backstamp, 16". (C)

Faience plaque of children on bridge, c. 1881. Lizzie Arnald, artist. Doulton Lambeth backstamp, 15". (C)

Faience plaque of two women by the sea, c. 1890. John Bennett, artist. Doulton Lambeth backstamp, 12". (B)

Marqueterie trumpet vase, c. 1910. Artist unknown. Doulton Marqueterie backstamp, 8". (*B*)

Marqueterie figural sweetmeat dish, c. 1890. Artist unknown. Doulton Marqueterie backstamp, 11.75". (*H*)

Marqueterie vase of child with gold bird handles, c. 1900. Artist unknown. Doulton Marqueterie backstamp, 8". (*B*)

143

Doulton Burslem

The Lambeth Art Studio was thriving when Henry Doulton began the next chapter in the Doulton story. In 1877 Doulton and Company formed a partnership with Pinder, Bourne and Company, a moderately successful earthenware manufacturer on Nile Street in Burslem, Staffordshire. Impressed by the remarkable success Henry Doulton had achieved at Lambeth, founder Thomas Shadford Pinder hoped that Doulton's financial investment and entrepreneurial skills would elevate his company to the level of other major Staffordshire potteries. Henry Doulton saw the partnership as his opportunity to begin earthenware manufacturing in the heart of British pottery production. Unfortunately their partnership was stormy and short lived.

After five years, Pinder retired from the business. Henry and his brother James became sole proprietors and renamed the company Doulton and Company. Henry was determined to make his new venture a success and took an active role in its management. No longer just a once-a-week visitor, Doulton spent an intensive six months at Burslem, personally investigating every aspect of production and marketing.

The decision was made to retain John Slater, a young, talented Art Director who had been trained at Minton. Henry

A Royal Doulton Burslem figure painter, 1913.

Doulton told his young protégé: "Forget, for Heaven's sake, most of what was done here in the past; we are going to make a new beginning and I intend, come what may, to bring the Burslem products up to the standards we have set at Lambeth." John Slater, along with the newly appointed general works manager, twenty-three-year old John Cuthbert Bailey, was entrusted with the task of establishing an art department.

Yet in spite of assistance from the Lambeth studio, the underglazed decorated earthenware produced at the Nile Street factory was pale in comparison with the china products being produced by other leading British potteries. Recognizing the earthenware's limitations, Slater and Bailey concluded that a fine translucent bone-china body had to be developed to showcase the skills of their talented artists.

The two gentlemen tried unsuccessfully to persuade Henry Doulton to build a china-works factory. Estimated to cost the exorbitant price of £25,000, the factory was promised to be the most up-to-date in Staffordshire. Doulton would not grant permission for a new factory until he was satisfied that the earthenware production was firmly established. Upon receiving a sizable North American order for new tableware designs in bone china, Slater and Bailey

Opposite page:
Henry Doulton (right) with Edward, the Prince of Wales, after receiving the distinguished Albert Medal of the Society Arts, 1885.

conspired to fill the order by secretly obtaining a supply of plain white glazed porcelain from Limoge of France. These pieces were decorated by the Nile Street artists and then accidentally marked "Doulton and Company."

While visiting the Burslem factory, Henry Doulton spotted the Limoge-painted pieces with their unauthorized Doulton trademark. Flying into an uncharacteristic fury, he smashed the pieces with his umbrella and immediately suspended Slater and Bailey telling them they would be reprimanded later. He stormed out of the studio planning to return to London. Fortunately, he missed his train, forcing him to spend the night at a hotel in Stoke-on-Trent.

A clay carrier at Royal Doulton, 1913.

During the night, Doulton recalled the artistic superiority displayed on the translucent porcelain. Already a wealthy man with more money than he would ever need, Doulton knew he could afford to patronize a new enterprise even if a profitable outcome was not assured. He realized that Slater and Bailey's aspirations arose from a sincere desire to enhance the name of Doulton.

The following morning Doulton returned to Nile Street to greet Bailey and Slater who feared that his return meant the end of the Burslem venture entirely. Doulton not only surprised the gentlemen with their reinstatement, but also announced the immediate building of a china studio at Nile Street.

In 1884, John Slater developed a superior china body—strong, white, and notably translucent. This necessitated the assembly of a larger group of artists, designers, modelers, gilders, and engravers. Many of the artists were already at Nile Street, having been trained in the art of china decoration at local schools or other factories like Minton, Derby, and Worcester. These artists included Robert Allen, Fred Hancock, William Hodkinson, Charles Yeomans, David Dewsberry, and Percy Curnock.

The fine earthenware body continued to be used for everyday tableware and inexpensive decorative pottery. The china body had been developed for the more expensive tableware, tea services, richly decorated fish and game plates, and lavishly hand-painted vases that were in great demand in the United States, Australia, and New Zealand.

The wares produced at the Burslem factory quickly gained a reputation for their superior quality and decorative appeal. Over the next few years, other well-known artists joined the ranks and the number of employees at Nile Street quickly rose from 160 in 1877 to over 500 in 1884.

In 1885, Henry Doulton was honored with an award formerly given to notables such as Louis Pasteur. The Albert Medal of the Society Arts was awarded to him for his outstanding leadership in the British pottery production as well as his role in promoting technical education and the employment of women. Adding to Doulton's pleasure in receiving the award was the fact that the Prince of Wales—England's future King Edward VII—presented the medal at Lambeth Headquarters where Henry Doulton's loyal employees could share in the honor. Henry was quick to acknowledge the importance of his employees in his success. As the first potter to receive the medal since its inception in 1863, Henry Doulton was rightfully proud of the honor. Another first occurred two years later when Henry was knighted—again the first potter to be titled "Sir."

In 1889, Doulton's most important artist joined the firm. Charles J. Noke, a trained modeler at the Royal Worcester Porcelain Works for sixteen years, came to Doulton "not for the money, but for the freedom and the promise." John Slater had seen his work at exhibitions and invited him to join the Doulton Company. Noke's special talents as a modeler were quickly realized, especially in his ornamental centerpieces and elaborate vases. He would later lay the foundation for Doulton's highly successful figure production in the 20th century.

Doulton's glazed and enameled terra cotta pavilion at the Glasgow Exhibition, 1888. The pavilion was designed by Arthur Pearce.

Doulton's assembly of so many talented artists was a first in the history of Staffordshire. Following the example of Henry Doulton's successful leadership at Lambeth, Slater and Bailey encouraged artists and apprentices to develop their own individual style. Inspiration came from the Baroque, Rococo, Neo-classical, and Oriental styles. Doulton artists brought their original approaches to landscape, floral, and figure painting and were allowed complete artistic freedom and the opportunity to create their own style of design.

By 1891, Henry Doulton was fully satisfied with the products that had been made at Nile Street and was ready to show the world what his Burslem Pottery could produce. The first prominent display of Burslem wares was staged at the Chicago Exhibition of 1893. Sir Philip Cunliffe-Owen, Director of the South Kensington Museum, described the Doulton display as "Henry Doulton's greatest triumph." Any remaining doubt as to whether Doulton's Burslem Pottery would repeat the success achieved at Lambeth was silenced in Chicago. Critics and public alike were impressed by the large prestigious exhibition pieces, including the "Dante" vase designed by Charles J. Noke as well as the "Diana" vase which stood five-foot high with a figure of the huntress at the summit and her dog at her feet.

At this great exhibition Charles J. Noke launched his new line of figures inspired by actors on the English stage. Regrettably, they were overshadowed by the larger, somewhat more impressive pieces. Noke's creations, ranging in size from 8-20 inches, were detailed in subtle shades of ivory, pink and green and then treated with a delicate parchment colored glaze known as "vellum." Robert Allan and his team of artists were responsible for painting lavishly detailed figures of Jack Point, the Moorish Minstrel, and the Lady Jester. Today, it is rare to find these vellum figures, indicating that they were made in limited editions and only for a short period.

The Doulton Pavilion, showcasing art wares from the Burslem and Lambeth studios, at the Chicago Exhibition, 1893.

Doulton and Company took seven of the highest awards at the exhibition, the largest number granted to any pottery firm. By the end of the 19th century, under the direction of Doulton, Slater, and Bailey, along with Charles J. Noke and the team of designers and artists, the Nile Street Pottery was regarded as one of the greatest in the world.

Unfortunately, Henry Doulton was experiencing failing health at the very time his company was being lauded. In 1896, he courageously underwent major surgery that he understood would give him only a brief amount of time. Yet it was time he wanted in order to continue his work. The following year on November 17, 1897, Henry Doulton died at his home in Kensington at the age of seventy-seven. Four years later the new King Edward VII presented the Doulton Company with the Royal Warrant of Appointment, bestowing the privilege of using the word ROYAL to describe Doulton products.

Charles J. Noke and later his son, Cecil, continued the success at the Burslem factory. Noke senior retired in 1936 and placed the reins in Cecil's hands. A much-loved administrator, Cecil oversaw a team of artists and designers from the Royal College of Art and other centers until his unexpected death in 1954.

This photograph, taken c. 1910, illustrates the vast amount of work being produced at the Burslem factory.

Woman artists decorating Doulton Burslem wares in the late 19th century.

George White

Left: Seabreeze vase; center: Maiden vase; right: The Dove vase, c. 1895-1905. George White, artist for all. Doulton Burslem backstamp on all, 11", 10.5", 10". (*E, F, F*)

Sleeping angel vase, c. 1895. George White, artist. Royal Doulton England backstamp, 17". (*I*)

Trio of three vases: girl with violin and two girls with flowers, c. 1880. George White, artist. Doulton Burslem backstamp, 15", 10". (T)

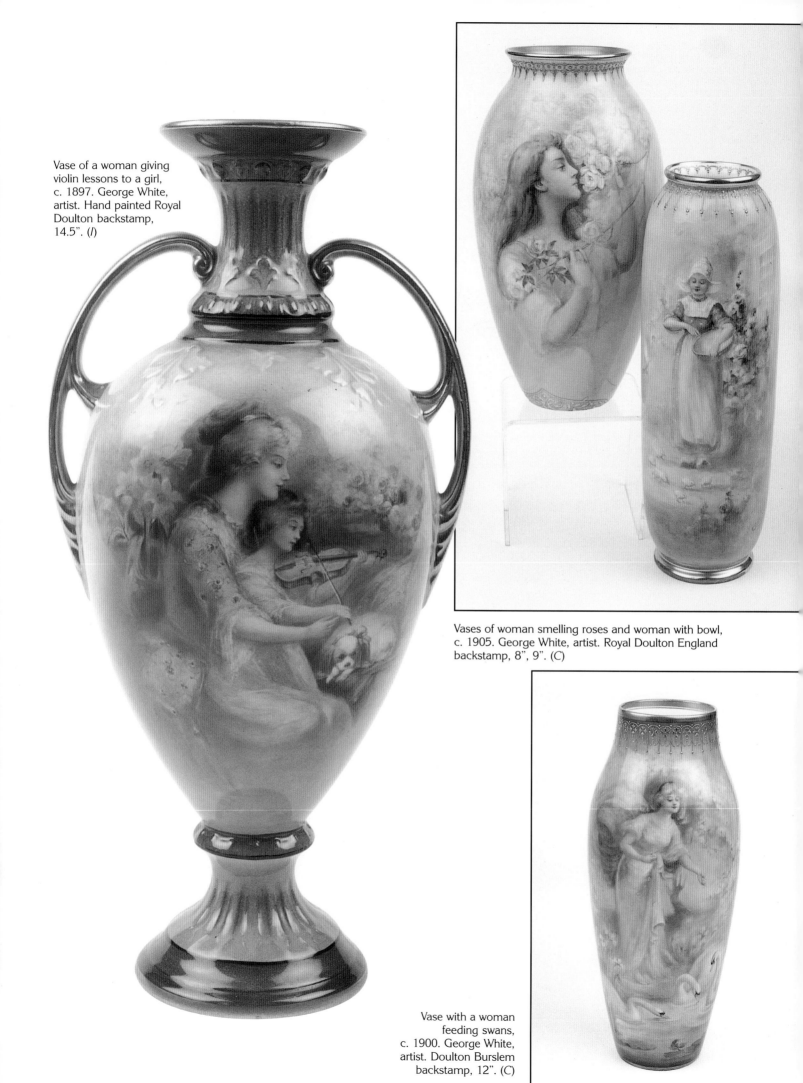

Vase of a woman giving violin lessons to a girl, c. 1897. George White, artist. Hand painted Royal Doulton backstamp, 14.5". (*I*)

Vases of woman smelling roses and woman with bowl, c. 1905. George White, artist. Royal Doulton England backstamp, 8", 9". (*C*)

Vase with a woman feeding swans, c. 1900. George White, artist. Doulton Burslem backstamp, 12". (*C*)

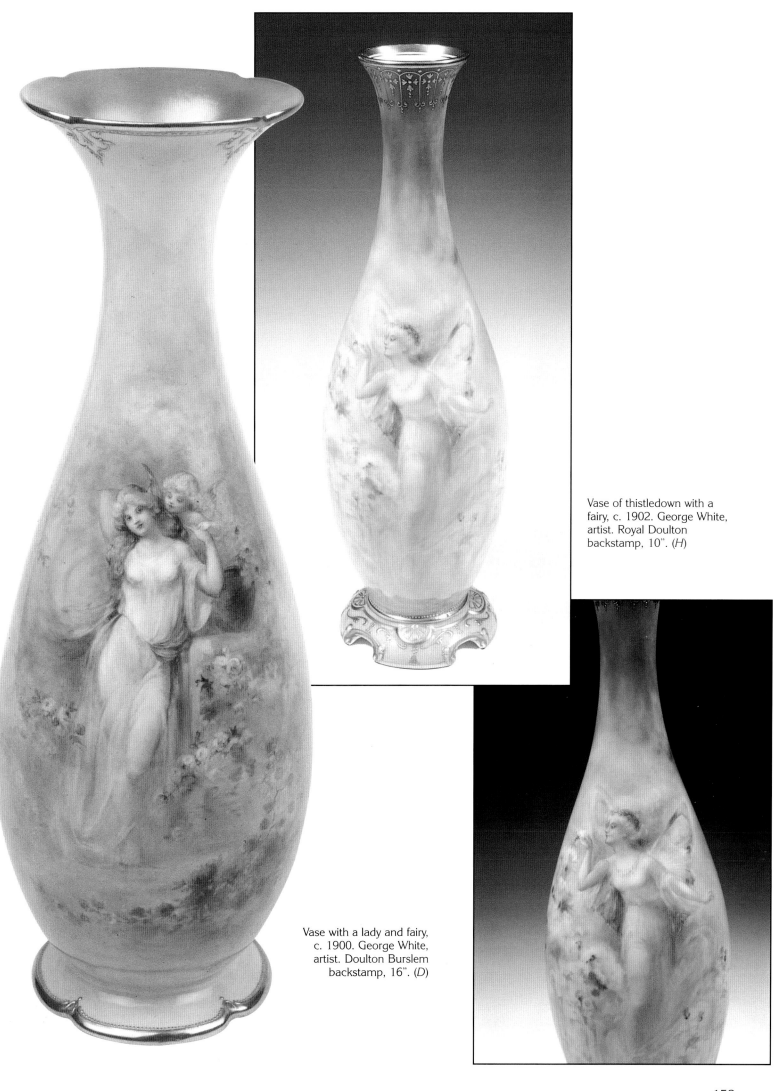

Vase of thistledown with a
fairy, c. 1902. George White,
artist. Royal Doulton
backstamp, 10". (*H*)

Vase with a lady and fairy,
c. 1900. George White,
artist. Doulton Burslem
backstamp, 16". (*D*)

Leslie Johnson

Oval plaque of a woman in a bonnet touching tree blossoms, c. 1890. Leslie Johnson, artist. Doulton Burslem backstamp, 8" x 6". (C)

Vase of a maiden, c. 1890. Leslie Johnson, artist. Doulton Burslem backstamp, 18.5". (T)

Oval plaque with two women at lakeside picnic, c. 1900. Leslie Johnson, artist. Doulton Burslem backstamp, 9" x 12". (C)

Plaque with a portrait of a lady, c. 1900. Leslie Johnson, artist. Doulton Burslem backstamp, 8" x 12". (C)

Round plaque of a woman wearing a bonnet, c. 1910. Leslie Johnson, artist. Doulton England backstamp, 4.5". (B)

155

Vase of a woman with tambourine and vase with a woman touching her neck, c. 1890. Leslie Johnson, artist. Doulton Burslem backstamp, 9", 10.5". (C)

Plaque of a boy on a sofa, c. 1920. Leslie Johnson, artist. Doulton England backstamp, 7" x 5". (B)

Oval plaque of a woman in a pink dress with a blue bonnet, c. 1890. Leslie Johnson, artist. Doulton Burslem backstamp, 8" x 6". (C)

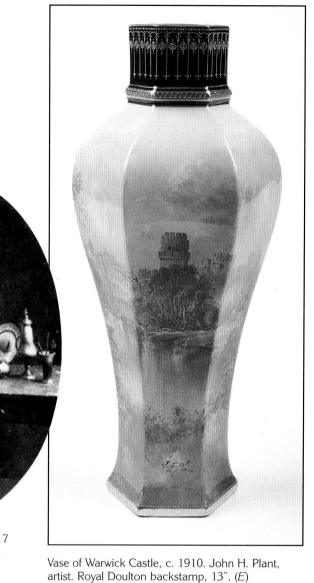

John Plant, 1902-1917

Vase of Warwick Castle, c. 1910. John H. Plant, artist. Royal Doulton backstamp, 13". (E)

Vase of Dryburgh Abbey, c. 1890. John H. Plant, artist. Doulton Burslem backstamp, 11". (C)

Pedestal vase with farm scene and lid, c. 1900. John H. Plant, artist. Royal Doulton England backstamp, 9". (B)

Pair of light blue vases with sea scenes, c. 1910. John H. Plant, artist. Royal Doulton backstamp, 11.25". (B)

H.G. Theaker

Pair of vases with women picking fruit; and a girl offering flowers, c. 1890. H.G. Theaker, artist. Doulton Burslem backstamp, 7.5". (*B*)

Vase with a woman on a tree branch, c. 1890. H.G. Theaker, artist. Doulton Burslem backstamp, 11". (*C*)

Vase with children portraits, c. 1890. H.G. Theaker, artist. Doulton Burslem backstamp, 11.5". (*A*)

Vase of ladies at rest, c. 1890. H.G. Theaker, artist. Doulton Burslem backstamp, 8". (*B*)

Vase of a girl smelling flowers with gold gilt handles, c. 1900. H.G. Theaker, artist. Doulton Burslem backstamp, 16". (*B*)

H. Allen

Pair of Arabian double-handled vases, c. 1905. H. Allen, artist. Royal Doulton England backstamp, 8". (*C* for pr.)

Arab man on vase, c. 1910. H. Allen, artist. Royal Doulton England backstamp, 9". (*B*)

Miniature vase with lid of Arab scene, c. 1915. H. Allen, artist. Royal Doulton England backstamp, 5.5". (*A*)

Pair of vases with mystical children, c. 1885. Henri Boullemier, artist. Doulton Burslem backstamp, 8.75". (C)

Vase with an Asian woman, c. 1890. Louis Bolton, artist. Doulton Burslem backstamp, 12". (C)

Pair of vases with seaside scenes, c. 1900. W. Brown, artist. Doulton Burslem backstamp, 6.75". (B)

Group of three vases with women, c. 1920. A. Dix, artist. Royal Doulton England backstamp, 10", 9", 8.5". (*B* ea.)

Vase of a maiden, c. 1900. A. Dix, artist. Doulton England backstamp, 8.5". (*B*)

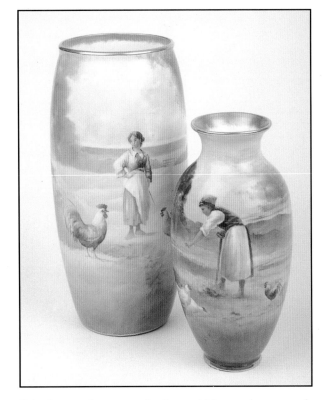

Pair of vases of a woman feeding a chicken and a man and a chicken, c. 1900. Percy Curnock, artist. Doulton Burslem backstamp, 8.5", 10.5". (*B*)

Percy Curnock, 1885-1954.

Vase with angel, c. 1905. C. Collins, artist. Royal Doulton England backstamp, 13". (*B*)

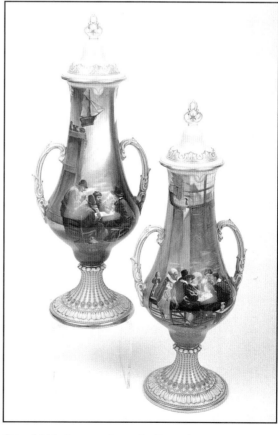

Pair of lidded vases of men in discussion, c. 1910. A. Eaton, artist. Royal Doulton England backstamp, 12". (*D*)

Vase with men in discussion, c. 1905. A. Eaton, artist. Royal Doulton England backstamp, 9". (*C*)

John Hancock

Pair of double-handled autumn scene vases,
c. 1910. John Hancock, artist. Royal Doulton
England backstamp, 11.75". (B)

Vase with ladies and a dog under a tree in bloom,
c. 1880. John Hancock, artist. Doulton Burslem
backstamp, 14.5". (D)

Vase with two girls in a field with a cow, c. 1910. John Hancock, artist. Royal Doulton England backstamp, 10.5". (C)

Pair of vases of "Rising Moon" and "Waning Moon," 1918. John Hancock, artist. Royal Doulton England backstamp, 13.5". (F)

Vase with farmers in a field, 1905. John Hancock, artist. Royal Doulton England backstamp, 13". (F)

165

This page:
Pair of ewers with women and children, c. 1890. L.P. Hewitt, artist. Doulton Burslem backstamp, 14". (*C*)

Vase with mermaids,
c. 1890. W.G.
Hodkinson, artist.
Doulton Burslem
backstamp, 12.5". (C)

Trio of farm scene vases, c. 1905. J. Hughs, artist. Royal
Doulton England backstamp, 8", 8.25", 9". (A ea.)

Vase with Arab scene in four panels,
c. 1915. Charles B. Hopkins, artist. Royal Doulton
England backstamp, 8.5". (B)

Charles B. Hopkins

This page:
Exhibition vase of cattle in a field, 1882. Charles B. Hopkins, artist. Doulton Burslem backstamp, 28". (*T*)

Miniature vase of a farm with a man plowing the field, c. 1920. H. Nixon, artist. Royal Doulton England backstamp, 4.5". (*A*)

Double-handled vase of a farmer plowing, c. 1920. H. Nixon, artist. Royal Doulton England backstamp, 8". (*A*)

Vase of animals in a pasture, 1890. Kelsall, artist. Doulton Burslem backstamp, 12". (*B*)

Pair of vases with a lady in a field of flowers, c. 1885.
Arthur Leslie, artist. Doulton Burslem backstamp, 12". (*D*)

Trio of vases, each with a lady, c. 1905. Arthur Leslie,
artist. Royal Doulton England backstamp, 8", 9", 12". (*F*)

Pair of vases with birds, c. 1890. S.
Wilson Pinet, artist. Doulton
Burslem backstamp, 7". (*A*)

Two lovers scenes with cherub handles, c. 1880. Artist unknown. Doulton Burslem backstamp, 17". (T)

Warwick Castle vase with reticulated lid, c. 1890. H. Morley, artist. Doulton Burslem backstamp, 17". (C)

Classic Falstaff vase, c. 1905. R. Johnson, artist. Royal Doulton England backstamp, 10.5". (B)

171

Both pages:
Dante exhibition vase, c. 1880. Charles J. Noke,
artist. Doulton Burslem backstamp, 36". (*T*)

Charles J. Noke.

174

Both pages::
Dante vase with portrait center and vellum figures, c. 1890. Charles J. Noke, artist. Doulton Burslem backstamp, 36". (*Q*)

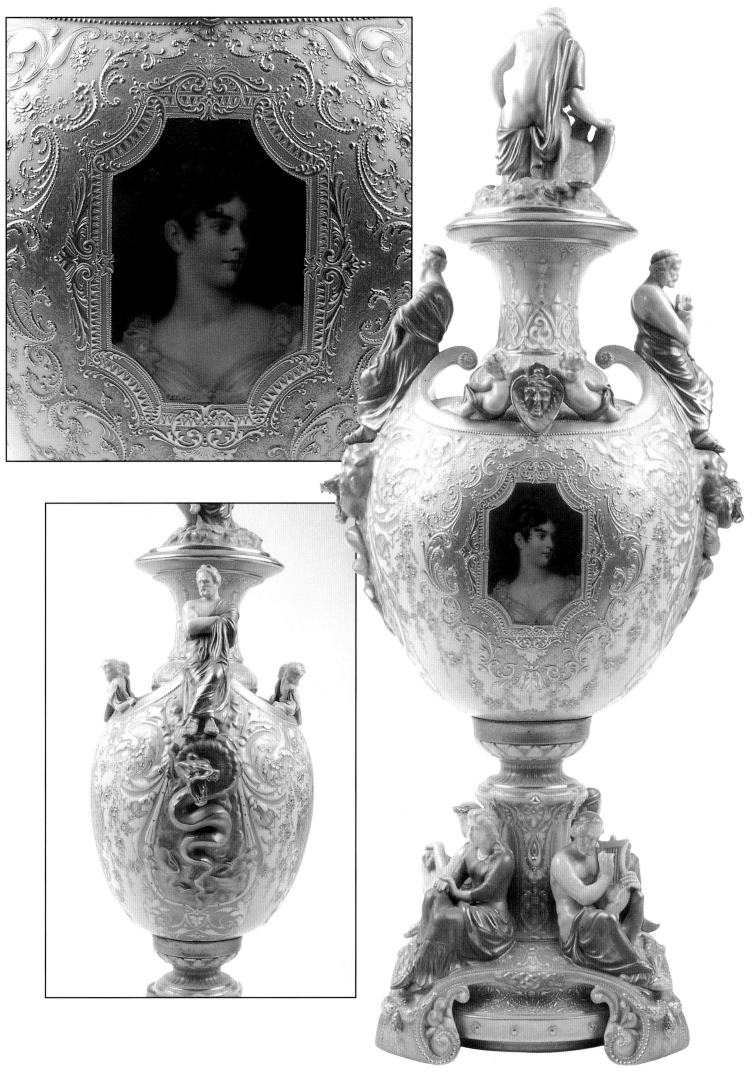

Walter Nunn

A trio of hand-painted vases with male characters, c. 1900. Walter Nunn, artist. Doulton Burslem backstamp, 12", 12", 18". (C)

Vase of a man with a walking stick, c. 1890. Walter Nunn, artist. Doulton Burslem backstamp, 12.5". (B)

Vase with a woman serving drinks to men in a tavern, c. 1900. Walter Nunn, artist. Royal Doulton Burslem backstamp, 11.5". (C)

Vase with a man toasting "The King," c. 1890. Walter Nunn, artist. Doulton Burslem backstamp, 11". (B)

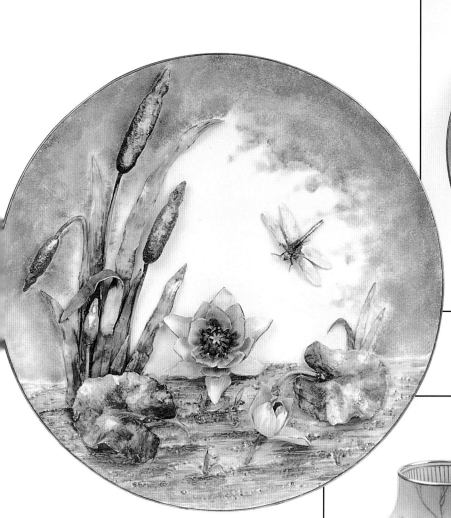

Pair of Doulton Burslem earthenware framed plaques, modeled in almost full relief with various plants and insects, c. 1882. J.H. Sale, artist. Doulton Burslem backstamp, 20". (*B*)

Floral vase with twisted gold handles, c. 1890. E. Turner, artist. Doulton Burslem backstamp, 9". (*A*)

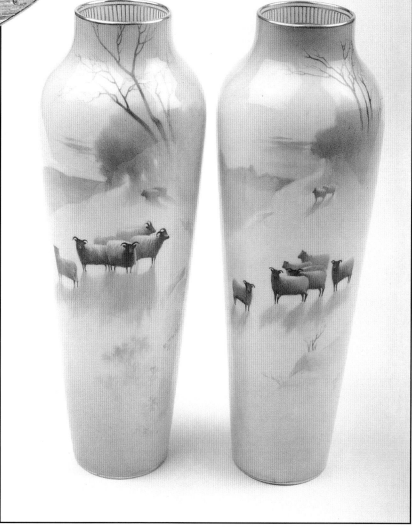

Pair of sheep vases, c. 1905. F. Walkett, artist. Royal Doulton backstamp, 8.5". (*B*)

177

Two-handled vessel with lid, "Discovery of the New World," c. 1900. Harry Tittensor, artist. Royal Doulton England backstamp, 12". (*T*)

Vase with a man playing a guitar, c. 1910. Harry Tittensor, artist. Doulton Burslem backstamp, 13.5". (*D*)

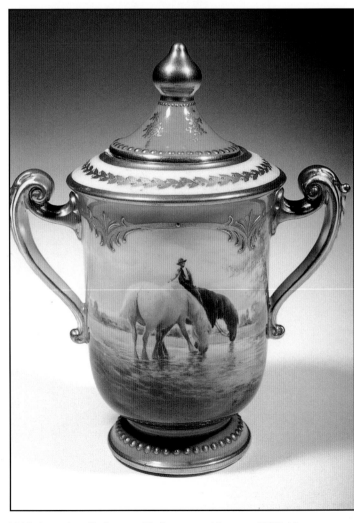

Lidded two-handled vase with farmer and horses, 1910. Harry Tittensor, artist. Doulton Burslem backstamp, 4". (*A*)

Fred Sutton

Vase of Catherine Howard, c. 1879. Fred
Sutton, artist. Doulton Burslem backstamp,
7". (*B*)

Double-handle vase
with a girl in a pink
tunic, c. 1890. Fred
Sutton, artist. Doulton
Burslem backstamp,
10". (*B*)

Pair of portrait vases of women, c. 1890.
Fred Sutton, artist. Doulton Burslem
backstamp, 8.25", 7.5". (*B*)

Portrait of a man with a peacock design on top of vase, c. 1905. Samuel Wilson, artist. Royal Doulton backstamp, 9". (B)

Vase with Egyptian woman scene with gilded flowers, c. 1890. Samuel Wilson, artist. Doulton Burslem backstamp, 12.5". (T)

Lidded vase with a woman in a pink dress holding a flower, c. 1890. S. Tushingham, artist. Doulton Burslem backstamp, 12". (C)

180

Classical figure playing the triangle, c. 1885. Artist unknown. Doulton Burslem backstamp, 4" x 14.5". (C)

Framed plaque of a man and a woman dancing, c. 1880. Artist unknown. Doulton Burslem backstamp, 4" x 6". (A)

Giant plaque of a mother holding a child, c. 1890. Artist unknown. Doulton Burslem backstamp, 22". (D)

181

Small sized plaque of woman with pearls, c. 1890. Artist unknown. Doulton Burslem backstamp, 5". (B)

Vase with a woman holding flowers, c. 1890. Artist unknown. Doulton Burslem backstamp, 9.5". (C)

Two vases in blue of women, c. 1890. Artist unknown. Doulton Burslem backstamp, 8", 9". (B)

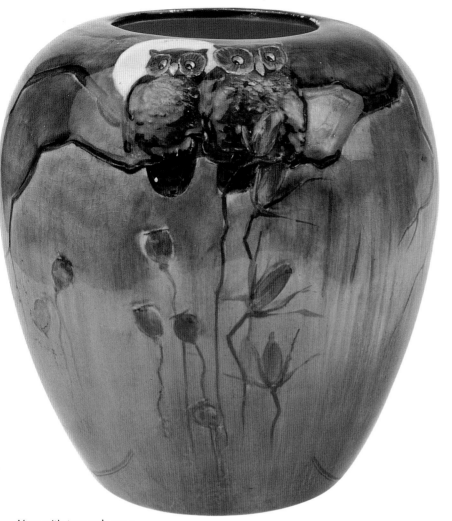

Vase with two owls on a branch in moonlight, c. 1900. Artist unknown. Royal Doulton England backstamp, 7.5". (B)

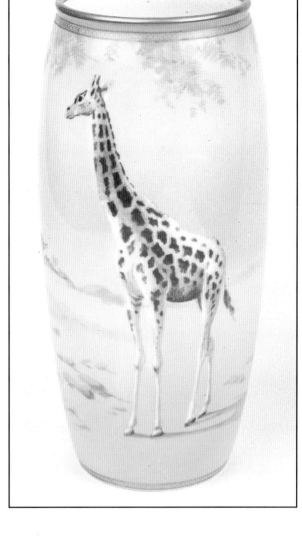

Giraffe vase, c. 1900. Artist unknown. Royal Doulton England backstamp, 10". (B)

Four Holbein ware vases with animal scenes, c. 1900. Artist unknown. Doulton Burslem backstamp, 10", 11.5". (B)

Jar and lid with a frog playing flute for a mouse, with Spanishware detail, 1885. Artist unknown. Doulton Burslem backstamp, 7". (R)

Decorated clock case with flowers, c. 1890. Artist unknown. Doulton Burslem backstamp, 14". (B)

Cherubs holding dish, c. 1880. Artist unknown. Doulton Burslem backstamp, 5". (A)

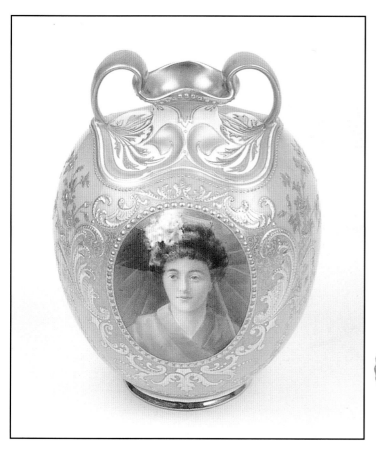

Vase with cameo of a woman, c. 1890. Artist unknown.
Doulton Burslem backstamp, 9". (C)

Vase with cameo of woman, c. 1890. Artist
unknown. Doulton Burslem backstamp, 9". (C)

Vase with cameo of a lady with flowers in her hair,
c. 1890. Artist unknown. Doulton Burslem
backstamp, 7". (B)

Trio of vases with gold dragon appliqués,
c. 1886. Artist unknown. Doulton Burslem
backstamp, 13", 11", 11". (C)

"Dragon Tusk" vases (wine vessels) with lids, c. 1880.
Artist unknown. Doulton Burslem backstamp, 14",
16". (E)

Spanishware floral vase with face panels,
c. 1880. Artist unknown. Doulton Burslem
backstamp, 15". (D)

Patê-sur-Patê

A patê-sur-patê vase and tyg,
c. 1890. A. Morgan, artist.
Doulton Burslem backstamp,
12.5", 6". (*Unknown*)

This page:
Vellum pitcher with floral panels and angel handle,
c. 1880. Artist unknown. Doulton Burslem
backstamp, 16". (C)

Vellum vase of woman with cupids, c. 1890.
Charles Labarre, artist. Doulton Burslem
backstamp, 13.5". (C)

Vellum vase with floral panel and
dragon handles, c. 1890. Louis
Bilton, artist. Doulton Burslem
backstamp, 20". (C)

Vellum vase of a woman in a yellow
headdress, 1880. Artist unknown. Doulton
Burslem backstamp, 14". (C)

Vellum vase with scrolls, faces, and floral painting, 1885.
Artist unknown. Doulton Burslem backstamp, 18". (C)

Vellum urn with Spanishware detail and gold gilt handles, 1880.
Artist unknown. Doulton Burslem backstamp, 17". (D)

Pair of Vellum vases with flowers and ornate lids, handles with maiden faces, c. 1880. Artist unknown. Doulton Burslem backstamp, 17". (*D*)

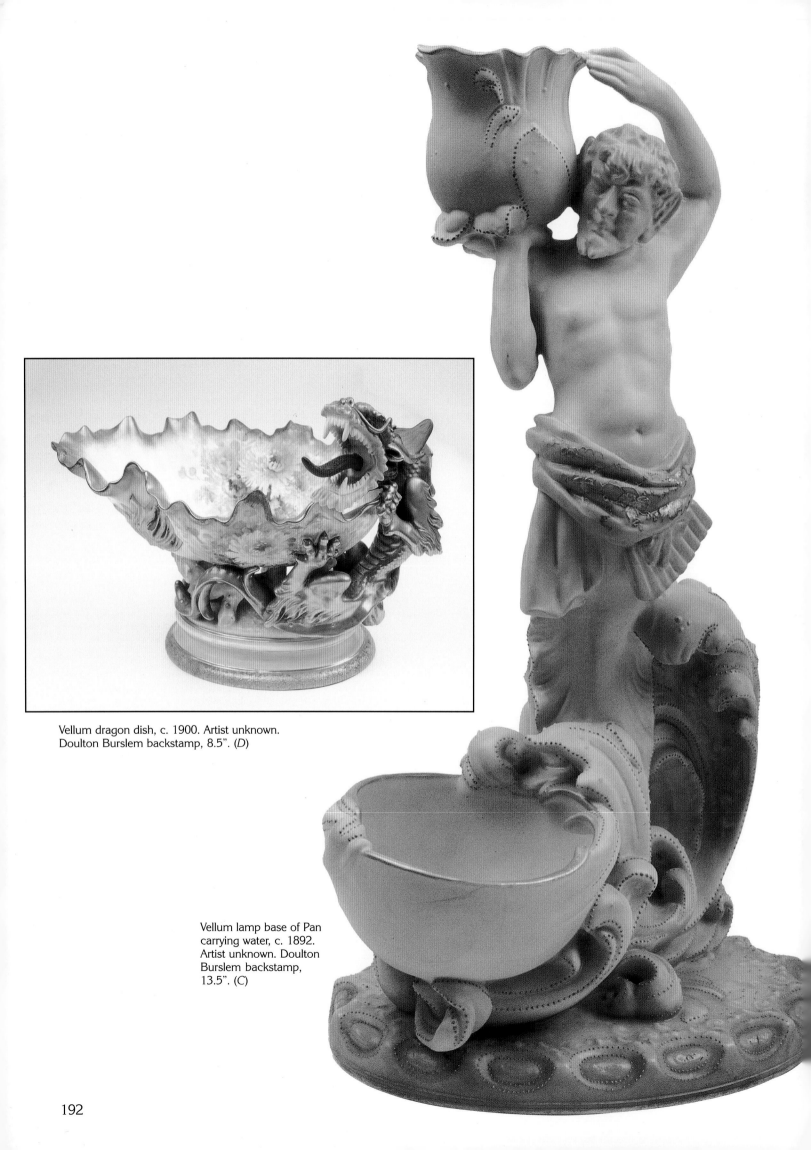

Vellum dragon dish, c. 1900. Artist unknown.
Doulton Burslem backstamp, 8.5". (*D*)

Vellum lamp base of Pan
carrying water, c. 1892.
Artist unknown. Doulton
Burslem backstamp,
13.5". (*C*)

This page:
Vellum figure, "Mirth and Melancholy," 1892. Charles J. Noke, artist. Doulton Burslem backstamp, 16". (*K*)

This page and opposite:
Vellum figural seashell centerpiece, c. 1880. Artist
unknown. Doulton Burslem backstamp, 24" x 23". (*F*)

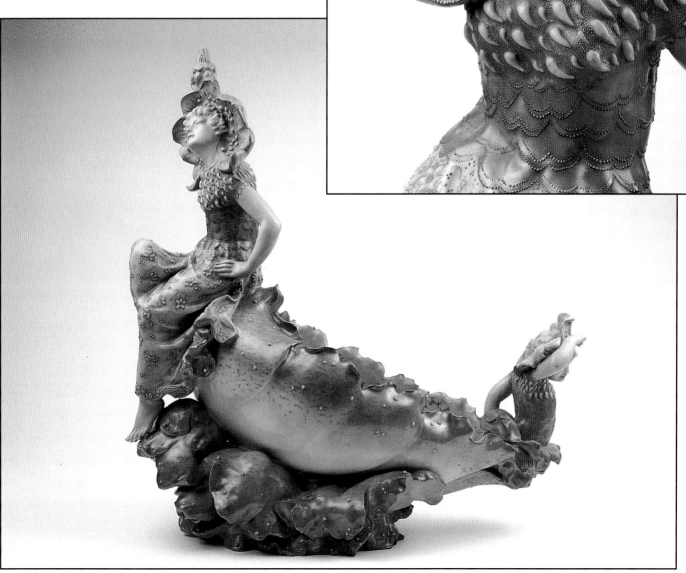

Vellum figure of Ellen Terry as Queen Catherine and Henry Irving as Cardinal Wolsey, c. 1880. Charles J. Noke, artist. Doulton Burslem backstamp, 12.5". (C)

Vellum figure of Henry Irving as Cardinal Wolsey and Ellen Terry as Queen Catherine, 1893. Charles J. Noke, artist. Doulton Burslem backstamp, 13". (C)

Vellum figure of Shylock and Portia, 1893.
Charles J. Noke, artist. Doulton Burslem
backstamp, 16". (T)

Entire page:
Vellum figure of Mephistopheles and Marguerite, 2 variations, 1891. Charles J. Noke, artist. Doulton Burslem backstamp, 12.5". (*E*)

Vellum figure of the Devil, 1893.
Charles J. Noke, artist. Doulton
Burslem backstamp, 19". (D)

"Oh Law!" double-sided Vellum figure, c. 1890. Charles J. Noke, artist. Doulton Burslem backstamp, 9.5". (*C*)

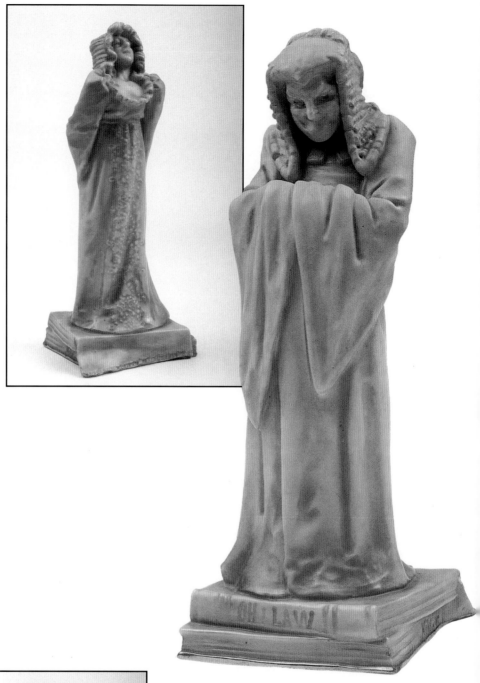

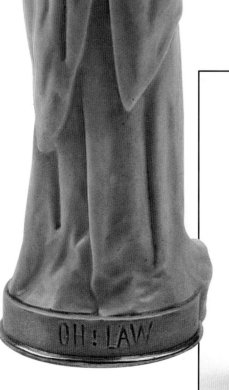

"Oh Law!," double-sided Vellum figure, 1893. Charles J. Noke, artist. Doulton Burslem backstamp, 8.5". (*D*)

Vellum figure of Cleopatra, c. 1880. Charles J. Noke, artist. Doulton Burslem backstamp, 12". (*E*)

Vellum figure of Shakespeare, 1899. Charles J. Noke, artist. Doulton Burslem backstamp, 12.5". (*D*)

Vellum figure of a Beefeater toasting the Queen, 1899. Charles J. Noke, artist. Doulton Burslem backstamp, 12.75". (*E*)

Vellum sorceress wall pocket, 1892. Charles J. Noke, artist. Doulton Burslem backstamp, 10.75". (*D*)

Vellum lady jester wall pocket, 1892. Charles J. Noke, artist. Doulton Burslem backstamp, 9.75". (*D*)

Vellum sorceress wall pocket (variation), Vellum, 1892. Charles J. Noke, artist. Doulton Burslem backstamp, 10.75". (*E*)

Vellum decorated dish with three legs, 1885. Artist unknown. Doulton Burslem backstamp, 4". (*A*)

Vellum Geisha wall pocket, 1893. Charles J. Noke, artist. Doulton Burslem backstamp, 9.25". (*C*)

Figure of the Kneeling Jester in an experimental glaze on Vellum, c. 1892. Charles J. Noke, artist. Doulton Burslem backstamp, 5.5". (*F*)

Classical figure
carrying a vase,
Vellum, c. 1890. Artist
unknown. Doulton
Burslem backstamp,
10". (C)

Lamp base of Moorish minstrel on Vellum,
1892. Charles J. Noke, artist. Doulton Burslem
backstamp, 12.5". (D)

Figure of the
Moorish minstrel in
an experimental
glaze of yellow and
green on Vellum,
1892. Charles J.
Noke, artist. Doulton
Burslem backstamp,
13". (D)

Jester lamp and two jester figures in
Vellum, 1892. Charles J. Noke, artist.
Doulton Burslem backstamp, Lamp:19"
(*H*); Figures: 9" (*G*).

Jester figure and lamp on Vellum, c.
1890. Charles J. Noke, artist. Doulton
Burslem backstamp, Figure: 9.5" (*C*);
Lamp: 10.5" (*D*).

SUNG

ROYAL DOULTON
OLD SUNG WARE

Flambé

In the late 1890s, European potters were experimenting to recreate the ancient Chinese art of high-temperature transmutation glazes. Chinese artists centuries earlier had learned to vary the amount of oxygen in the kiln at appropriate stages of firing while adding copper oxide and other organic substances. Even in China, the recipes for these brilliant colored glazes had largely been forgotten.

Armed with little technical information, Royal Doulton Art Director, John Slater, and his companion, Charles J. Noke, were determined to unravel the mystery of what French collectors of Chinese pottery generically called "flambé." By 1900, a few good pieces had been produced in the Doulton Factory but these men were far from being able to consistently produce the desired effect. The cost and unpredictability of the process left little hope for a commercially viable addition to the expanding Doulton range.

The necessary breakthrough came in 1902 when Cuthbert Bailey (son of John Cuthbert Bailey) and Bernard Moore joined their team. Bailey, a brilliant and respected ceramic chemist, brought his scientific approach to the group. His expertise lay in the technical aspects of pottery production and the construction of improved kilns. Moore, a young Staffordshire potter, had already achieved success with unusual glazes and was the first Englishman to successfully produce the flambé glaze.

Encouraged by Henry Doulton to continue their experiments, this team of four formed a unique partnership combining technical expertise, scientific knowledge and a shared enthusiasm supported by Doulton's financial backing. In the quest to master the flambé glaze, special kilns were built, countless experiments with different compositions and glazes were conducted, and a multitude of trial pieces were analyzed. Over three hundred shapes and sizes of vases, bowls, ashtrays, figures and animals emerged from the kilns covered in the glowing red glaze.

First shown at the 1904 St. Louis Exhibition, Royal Doulton flambé received universal praise and admiration. The Doulton studio won an unprecedented thirty awards, including two Grand Prix and four gold medals. The flambé range was favorably compared to Chinese originals and Arthur V. Rose, an expert on Oriental art, proclaimed the glaze to have "everything that the most enthusiastic collector could desire."

When Cuthbert Bailey left Doulton in 1907, Charles J. Noke took over responsibility for the further development and technical research of the transmutation glazes. His goal was to extend flambé's range of colors and textures and to control the veined effects on some of the earlier flambé wares. Noke experimented with those of his own figures that were particularly appropriate for the Oriental style glazes: One of the Forty, A Spook, and the Carpet Vendor.

✤ ✤ ✤ ✤ ✤ ROUGE FLAMBE ✤ ✤ ✤ ✤ ✤

✤ ✤ ✤ ✤ ✤ CHANG ✤ ✤ ✤ ✤ ✤

✤ ✤ ✤ ✤ ✤ SUNG ✤ ✤ ✤ ✤ ✤

A page from a Royal Doulton product brochure, c. 1926.

Another great achievement by Charles J. Noke came in 1919 with the development of "Sung" flambé wares, characterized by bright yellows, purples, oranges, and blues mottled beneath the flambé glaze. This was a bi-product of early flambé experiments: additional colors had appeared during firings and a range was created around these colorful "accidents." The magnificent Sung glazes can be found on the Smiling Buddha, the Jester, and the Moorish Piper Minstrel, as well as on elephants and other animal models. Various sized vases and bowls were decorated with exotic birds. Doulton's premier artists Harry Nixon, Arthur Eaton, and Fred Moore hand painted Sung wares with lavish images of fire-breathing dragons, snakes striking at unsuspecting birds, and tropical fish swimming in underwater scenes.

A lidded Sung ginger jar featured in a promotional brochure, 1925.

In 1925, Charles J. Noke, along with his son Cecil and Harry Nixon launched another remarkable ceramic innovation, "Chang Ware." Named after the ancient Chinese potter, Chang the Elder, these wares had a heavier body in order to withstand the contraction of several layers of thick, brilliantly colored glaze. This glaze, flowing like lava, was allowed to run and crackle down the piece offering limitless decorative effects. The kiln's unpredictability was exploited so that crazing became a characteristic of the Chang glaze. Consequently, no two pieces were alike. Nothing like it had been produced before, even in ancient China.

Noke's most impressive Chang piece, combining his modeling expertise and his fascination with animals, featured a realistically modeled dragon snaking menacingly around the body of a vase. The brilliant colors of blues, greens, reds, and purples contrasted with the uneven flow of the thick, sooty glazes. The Potter lamp, fired in 1930, is representative Chang with thick glaze creeping down the treetops covering the potter below. It represents the only figural example of Chang.

Interest in Chang flambé began to wane in the late 1930s when consumer tastes changed and it was no longer considered a novelty. Like the other transmutation glazes, including Chinese Jade and Titanian, Chang was only produced until the Second World War when luxury productions could no longer be justified. Restrictions on decorative china meant that the production of Chang flambé pieces virtually ended.

Today Royal Doulton's flambé and other transmutation glazes are admired and desired throughout the art world. Their unique characteristics assure a constant demand among collectors.

A promotional insert for "The Illustrated London News," c. 1925. This page was
part of special section on British Industry highlighting the wares being produced
at the Doulton Burslem factory.

Boy on crocodile, c. 1925. Charles J. Noke, artist.
Royal Doulton backstamp, 14". (*T*)

Left and below:
Alligator, c. 1920. Charles J. Noke, artist.
3" x 8". (*D*)

Monkey with dunce cap, unrecorded, c. 1928. Charles J. Noke, artist. Royal Doulton Flambé backstamp, 6". (T)

Peddler wolf figure, c. 1923. Charles J. Noke, artist. Royal Doulton England backstamp, 5.5". (D)

Owl candleholder with silver mount, c. 1920. Artist unknown. Royal Doulton Flambé backstamp, 7.75". (T)

211

Cat with mouse on tail, 1920. Charles J. Noke, artist. Royal Doulton backstamp, 4.5". (A)

Owl with owlet under wing, 1912. Charles J. Noke, artist. Royal Doulton Flambé backstamp, 4.75". (B)

Bison figure, 1929. Artist unknown. Royal Doulton backstamp, 4". (C)

Large elephant with trunk down, c. 1922. Charles J. Noke, artist.
Royal Doulton Flambé backstamp, 13". (C)

Herron in the marsh, 1921. Artist
unknown. Royal Doulton
backstamp, 5.5". (B)

Pair of jars with fox lids, c. 1920. Charles J. Noke, artist. Royal
Doulton Flambé backstamp, 7". (B)

Fox in hunting dress, c. 1940. Artist unknown. No backstamp, 8". (D)

Pig bowl with silver rim, c. 1920. Artist unknown. Royal Doulton Flambé backstamp, 1.75". (B)

Pair of bird speaker covers, c. 1920. Artist unknown. "Manufactured for Artandia Ltd. by Doulton & Company" backstamp, 15". (D)

Pair of vases with silver overlay, c. 1920. Artist unknown. Royal Doulton Flambé backstamp, 10.5", 5.75". (B)

Sitting lion on base, c. 1920. Charles J. Noke, artist. Royal Doulton England backstamp, 7". (*C*)

"Cockatoo," 1912. Leslie Harradine, artist. Royal Doulton Flambé backstamp, 6.5". (*A*)

Vessels with silver overlay, c. 1935. Charles J. Noke, artist. Doulton Flambé, 7", 8". (*B*)

Flambé St. George figure, c. 1925. S. Thorogood, artist. Royal
Doulton backstamp, 13.5". (*T*)

Laughing Buddha with figures on hand, c. 1925. Charles J. Noke, artist. 6". (*D*)

Pair of small Buddhas, c. 1920. Charles J. Noke, artist. Royal Doulton Flambé backstamp, 4". (*T*)

Jester and kneeling jester, c. 1925. Charles J. Noke, artist. Royal Doulton England backstamp, 9.5", 5.5". (C)

Trio of figures: Carpet Vendor; Carpet Vendor; One of Forty, c. 1925. Charles J. Noke, artist. Royal Doulton backstamp, 6", 6.25", 6.5". (T)

Moorish piper minstrel, c. 1920. Charles J. Noke, artist. Royal Doulton England backstamp, 14.5". (D)

Nude figure on rock, c. 1925. Artist unknown. Royal Doulton backstamp, 5". (C)

Old woman figure, c. 1920. Charles J. Noke, artist. Royal Doulton Flambé, 4.5". (T)

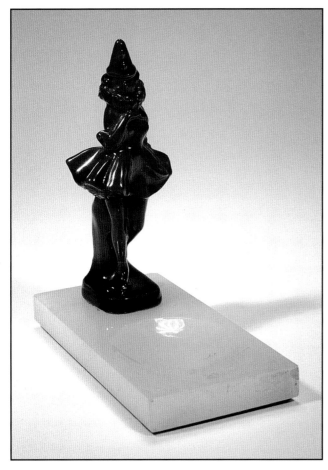

Miniature Pierrette figure on marble base, c. 1920. Artist unknown. No backstamp, 4.75". (B)

Prototype figure of wiseman, c. 1920. Artist unknown. Royal Doulton Flambé, 6.25". (F)

"Low Tide" vase, 1945. Harry Nixon, artist. Doulton Flambé backstamp, 16". (*G*)

"The Gleaners" vase with a cottage scene, 1938. Wilmot Brown, artist. Flambé backstamp, 17". (*D*)

Vase with landscape of mountains, c. 1920. Charles J. Noke and Fred Allen, artists. Doulton Flambe backstamp, 17". (T)

Vase with warriors on horses, c. 1920. Charles J. Noke and Arthur Eaton, artists. Doulton Flambé backstamp, 17". (*T*)

Vase with landscape of Venice, "Santa Marie Della Glate," c. 1920. Artist unknown. Doulton Flambé backstamp, 22". (*T*)

Vase with Egyptian sphinx and
pyramid, c. 1920. Artist unknown.
Doulton Flambé backstamp, 11". (*E*)

"Pride of Lions" vase, c. 1920.
Charles J. Noke and Arthur
Eaton, artists. Doulton Flambé
backstamp, 12". (*D*)

Ginger jar of a farm scene with cows, c. 1940. Fred
Moore and John Dennison, artists. Flambé
backstamp, 21". (*T*)

223

Vase with a medieval woman, c. 1925. Charles J. Noke and Arthur Eaton, artists. Flambé backstamp, 16". (*E*)

Vase with ravens in flight, 1933. Harry Nixon, artist. 7". (*B*)

Fruit vase, c. 1925. Harry Nixon, artist. Royal Doulton backstamp, 7". (*B*)

Vase with fish in turquoise and flambé, c. 1912. Artist unknown. Doulton Flambé backstamp, 9.5". (B)

Vase with sea scene, c. 1925. Charles J. Noke and Fred Allen, artists. Flambé backstamp, 18". (D)

Pair of vases, one with turquoise serpent, c. 1925. Artist unknown. Royal Doulton Flambé/Royal Doulton backstamp, 6.75", 4.5". (B)

Pair of six-sided Alchemist vases, c. 1928. Artist unknown.
Royal Doulton backstamp, 7.75". (C)

Vase with undersea scene,
c. 1920. Charles J. Noke,
artist; Fred Allen, assistant.
Royal Doulton Sung
backstamp, 7.25". (B)

Bernard Moore.

Vase with firebird design, 1925. Bernard
Moore, artist. Doulton Flambé England
backstamp, 17". (T)

Sung Flambé

Large Sung polar bear; and
cub with small Sung polar bear,
c. 1920. Charles J. Noke,
artist. Royal Doulton Sung
backstamp, 13.5", 6.5" . *(E&C)*

Above and right:
Large Sung polar bear and cub, c. 1920. Charles J. Noke,
artist. Royal Doulton Sung backstamp, 13.5". *(E)*

227

Two Sung figures of apes and monkey with hand to ear, c. 1913. Leslie Harradine, artist. Sung backstamp, 5", 3". (*T*)

Owl with owlet in Sung glaze, c. 1920. Charles J. Noke, artist. Royal Doulton Flambé backstamp, 5". (*B*)

Owl miniature in Sung glaze, 1948. Charles J. Noke, artist. Royal Doulton backstamp, 3.25". (*B*)

Pair of large fighting elephants (one Sung), c. 1925. Charles J. Noke, artist. Royal
Doulton/Royal Doulton Sung backstamp, 12". (*B & C*)

Pair of small elephants with tusks to side (one Sung), c. 1925. Charles J. Noke and Fred Allen,
artists. Royal Doulton/Royal Doulton Sung backstamp, 11". (*B & C*)

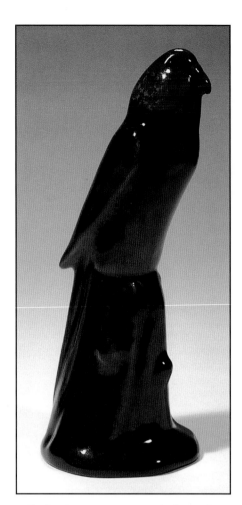

Budgerigar on tree stump in Sung glaze, 1918. Artist unknown. Royal Doulton England backstamp, 6.75". (A)

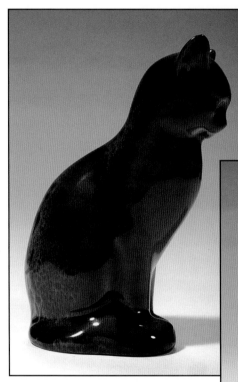

Sung sitting cat, c. 1920. Charles J. Noke, artist. Royal Doulton Sung backstamp, 4.5". (T)

Comic brown bear in Sung glaze, c. 1920. Artist unknown. Royal Doulton Flambé backstamp, 5.5". (B)

Experimental cat, c. 1920. Charles J. Noke, artist. Royal Doulton Flambé backstamp, 4.5". (T)

Above and right:
Pair of foxes leaning forward (one Sung), c. 1912. Charles J. Noke and Fred Allen, artists. Royal Doulton Sung backstamp, 4.75". (*A*)

Left and above:
Pair of sitting polar bears (one in Sung), 1912. Artist unknown. Royal Doulton England, 3.5". (*B*)

Buddha in Sung Flambé, 1920. Charles J. Noke, artist. Doulton Sung backstamp, 6". (C)

Jester in Sung Flambé, c. 1915. Charles J. Noke, artist. Doulton Sung backstamp, 6". (D)

Pair of Sung Buddha figures, c. 1925. Charles J. Noke, artist. Royal Doulton Sung backstamp, 7". (T)

Flambé spook figure, c. 1920. Charles J. Noke, artist. Royal Doulton backstamp, 7". (D)

232

Pair of gnome figures (one Sung,
c. 1925, one Titanian, 1920). Harry Tittensor,
artist. Royal Doulton backstamp, 5", 4". (*T*)

Mushroom on base in Sung glaze,
c. 1925. Artist unknown. Doulton
Flambé backstamp, 3". (*B*)

Sung Buddha speaker
cover, c. 1920. Charles J.
Noke, artist. Doulton and
Company Limited
backstamp, 13.5". (*E*)

Sung dish with mummy heads, c. 1920. Artist unknown. Sung backstamp, 5.75" x 3". (*T*)

Small Sung jar with lid, c. 1920. Artist unknown. Royal Doulton Sung backstamp, 5". (*B*)

Trio of Sung globular vases, c. 1920. Artist unknown. Royal Doulton Sung backstamp, 6.5", 7.25", 5". (*B*)

Plaques with Middle Eastern scenes, c. 1920. Charles J. Noke and Arthur Eaton, artists. Doulton Flambé backstamp, 9". (*C*)

Plaques with firebirds, c. 1920. Charles J. Noke, artist. Doulton Flambé England backstamp, 9". (*C*)

Sung two-handled Firebird bowl, c. 1920. Charles J. Noke and Arthur Eaton, artists. Doulton Flambé backstamp, 12". (*C*)

Snake and bird bowl, c. 1920. Charles J. Noke, artist. Royal Doulton Sung backstamp, 6" x 13". (C)

Shallow bowl with forest scene, c. 1920. Artist unknown. Royal Doulton Flambé backstamp, 3.5" h. x 14" l. (B)

Sung jar with elephant lid, c. 1920. Fred Moore, artist. Royal Doulton Sung backstamp, 6.5".

Colorful Sung dragon jar with lid, c. 1920. Artist unknown.
Royal Doulton Sung backstamp, 22". (*T*)

Sung dragon vase, c. 1920. Charles J. Noke and Arthur
Eaton, artists. Doulton Flambé backstamp, 13". (T)

Firebird Sung vase, c. 1920. Charles J. Noke,
artist. Doulton Flambé backstamp, 16". (G)

Dragon vase, c. 1920. Charles J. Noke, artist. Royal
Doulton Sung backstamp, 9.5". (T)

Firebird Sung vase, c. 1925. Charles J. Noke, artist. Flambé backstamp, 18". (*E*)

Sung peacock vase, c. 1920. Charles J. Noke and Arthur Eaton, artists. Doulton Flambé backstamp, 13". (*D*)

Sung Firebird vase, 1928. Charles J. Noke, Arthur Eaton, Fred Moore and Harry Nixon, artists. Doulton Flambé backstamp, 28". (*T*)

239

Vase of a peacock standing with flowers, c. 1925. Charles J. Noke, artist. Flambé backstamp, 15". (*T*)

Sung vase of ducks in flight, c. 1925. Charles J. Noke, artist. Flambé backstamp, 13". (*D*)

Firebird Sung vase, c. 1920. Charles J. Noke, artist. Doulton Flambé backstamp, 15". (*F*)

Vase with fighting eagles, c. 1925. Charles J. Noke, artist. Flambé backstamp, 15". (*T*)

Sung Firebird ginger jar, 1947. Charles J. Noke, Fred Moore, and D.G. Bensword, artists. Flambé backstamp, 21". (*T*)

Sung snake vase, c. 1930. Charles J. Noke and Arthur Eaton, artists. Doulton Flambé backstamp, 10". (*D*)

Peacock and snake Sung vase, c. 1920. Charles J. Noke, artist. Doulton Flambé backstamp, 17". (*T*)

Sung vase with wolves, c. 1930. Charles J. Noke, artist. Doulton Flambé England backstamp, 11". (*D*)

Sung eagle vase, c. 1920. Charles J. Noke, artist. Flambé backstamp, 18". (*G*)

Sung ducks in flight, c. 1925. Charles J. Noke and Arthur Eaton, artists. Flambé backstamp, 15". (*E*)

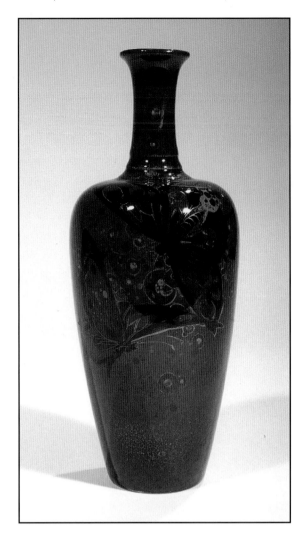

Sung butterfly vase, 1925. Charles J. Noke, artist.
Doulton Flambé backstamp, 8.5". (*C*)

Sung parrot vase,
c. 1925. Charles
J. Noke, artist.
Flambé
backstamp, 14".
(*T*)

Flamingo vase, c. 1920. Charles J. Noke, artist.
Royal Doulton Sung backstamp, 20". (*T*)

Sung deer vase, c. 1920. Artist unknown. Doulton Flambé backstamp, 10". (*T*)

Sung deer vase, c. 1920. Charles J. Noke, artist. Royal Doulton Sung backstamp, 7". (*C*)

Sung vase of deer in forest, 1928. Charles J. Noke and Arthur Eaton, artists. Doulton Flambé backstamp, 19". (*T*)

Underwater scene with fish in Sung glaze, c. 1920. Charles J. Noke, artist. Doulton Flambé backstamp, 13". (*T*)

Sung frog vase and bowl, c. 1920. Artist unknown. Royal Doulton Sung backstamp, vase: 5.25"; bowl: 2" x 5". (*B*)

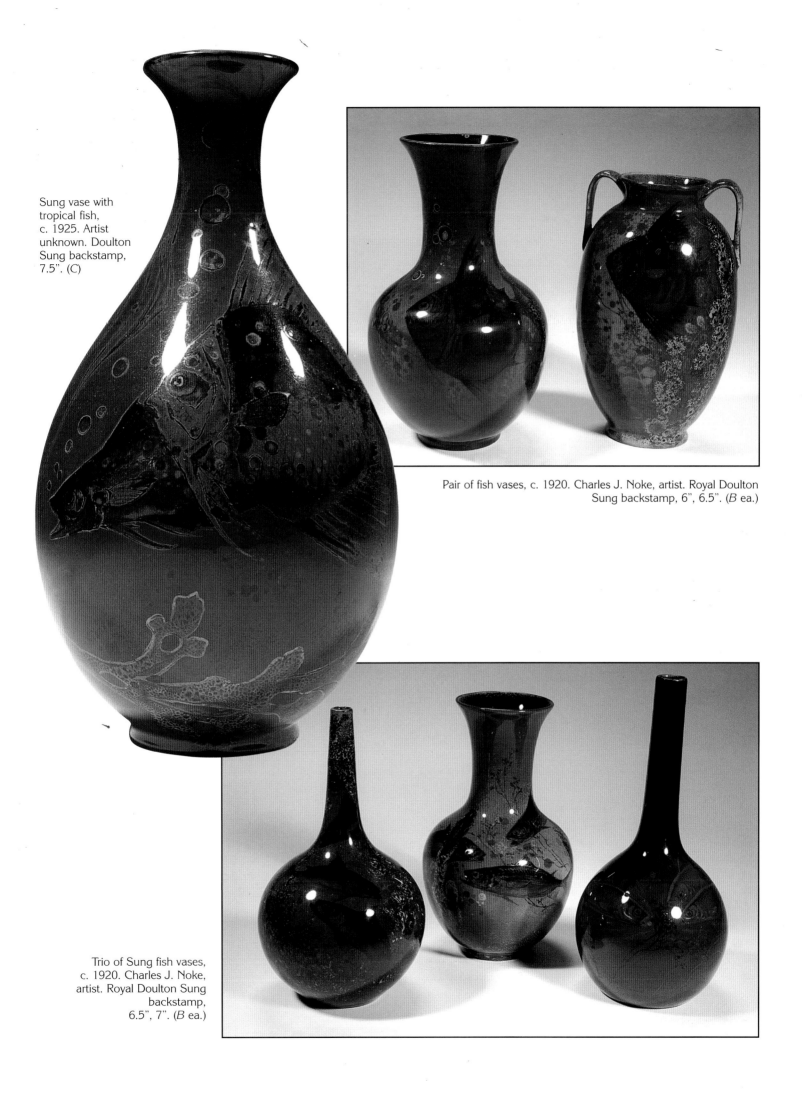

Sung vase with tropical fish, c. 1925. Artist unknown. Doulton Sung backstamp, 7.5". (C)

Pair of fish vases, c. 1920. Charles J. Noke, artist. Royal Doulton Sung backstamp, 6", 6.5". (B ea.)

Trio of Sung fish vases, c. 1920. Charles J. Noke, artist. Royal Doulton Sung backstamp, 6.5", 7". (B ea.)

Sung vase of cows drinking at sunset, 1925. Arthur Eaton, artist. Doulton Flambé England backstamp, 12". (T)

"Sunset Over Mountain Range" Sung vase, c. 1920. Charles J. Noke, artist. Doulton Flambé backstamp, 13". (C)

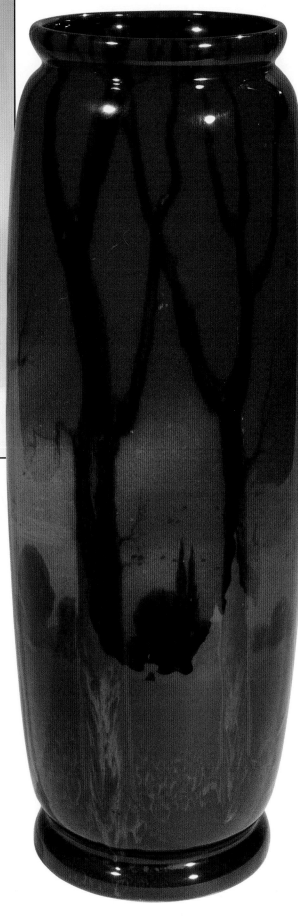

Sung forest scene vase, c. 1929. Charles J. Noke, artist. Doulton Flambé backstamp, 17". (F)

Sung vase with poppies, c. 1925. Charles J. Noke and Arthur Eaton, artists. Flambé backstamp, 9". (C)

"Trail through the forest" Sung vase, c. 1920. Charles J. Noke, artist. Doulton Flambé backstamp, 13". (D)

Sung vase with sheep herder, c. 1920. Charles J. Noke, artist. Royal Doulton Sung backstamp, 15". (T)

Lion vase, c. 1920. Charles J. Noke, artist. Royal Doulton Sung backstamp, 6.75. (*E*)

Firebird Sung vase, c. 1925. Charles J. Noke, artist. Flambé backstamp, 18". (*E*)

Sung ducks in flight, c. 1925. Charles J. Noke and Arthur Eaton, artists. Flambé backstamp, 15". (*E*)

Sung vase with lake, trees, and stream, 1928. Charles J. Noke and Arthur Eaton, artists. Doulton Flambé backstamp, 14". (C)

Sung scenic vase, c. 1925. Charles J. Noke and Arthur Eaton, artists. Doulton Flambé backstamp, 10". (D)

Portrait of a lady, c. 1920. Artist unknown.
Flambé backstamp, 12". (C)

Sung vase with two
women with
baskets, c. 1930.
Artist unknown.
Doulton Flambé
backstamp, 11".
(D)

Sung miniature pumpkin vase, 1915.
Charles J. Noke, artist. Royal Doulton
Flambé backstamp,4.75". (B)

Large Sung pumpkin vase, 1925. Charles
J. Noke, artist. Royal Doulton Flambé
backstamp,9.5". (B)

Sung miniature pumpkin vase, 1920. Charles J.
Noke, artist. Doulton Flambé backstamp,4.75". (B)

Sung alchemist vase, c. 1920. Charles J. Noke, artist. Doulton Flambé backstamp, 17". (T)

Sung alchemist vase, c. 1920. Charles J. Noke, artist. Doulton Flambé backstamp, 19". (T)

Sung vase with gnomes under a tree with mushrooms, 1925. Charles J. Noke, artist. Doulton Flambé backstamp, 6". (C)

Sung vase with gnomes under mushrooms, 1922. Charles J. Noke, artist. Flambé backstamp, 9.5". (T)

Vase with Pan and animals, c. 1925. Charles J. Noke, artist. Royal Doulton Sung backstamp, 20". (T)

Sung Gnome vase, c. 1920. Charles J. Noke, artist. Royal Doulton Sung backstamp, 5". (T)

254

Large Sung vase with Pan and animals, c. 1920.
Charles J. Noke and Arthur Eaton, artists. Royal
Doulton Sung backstamp, 25". (*T*)

Chang potter lamp, c. 1925. Charles J. Noke, artist. Chang backstamp, 11". (*T*)

Chang flambé vase
with dragon, c. 1920.
Charles J. Noke, artist.
Chang backstamp, 8".
(T)

Group of Chang vases, c. 1920. Charles J. Noke, artist.
Royal Doulton Chang backstamp, 5" - 9". (T)

Two Chang flambé vases, c. 1925. Charles J. Noke and Harry Nixon, artists. Chang backstamp, 5.25", 7.5". (C)

Chang elephant vase, c. 1925. Charles J. Noke, artist. Chang backstamp, 3.5". (B)

Chang vase, c. 1925. Charles J. Noke and Harry Nixon, artists. Chang backstamp, 15". (C)

Chang and Sung ashtrays, c. 1925. Charles J. Noke and Fred Moore, artists. Royal Doulton Chang/Royal Doulton Sung backstamps, 3.5" x 1.75" (B)

Chang vase, c. 1925. Charles J. Noke and Harry Nixon, artists. Royal Doulton Chang backstamp, 9.5". (*C*)

Chang flambé vase, c. 1920. Charles J. Noke, artist. Chang backstamp, 17". (*I*)

Large Chang flambé centerpiece bowl, c. 1925. Charles J. Noke, artist. Chang backstamp, 16" x 5.5". (*D*)

Titanian

Even though his Chang and Sung Flambé wares were receiving rave reviews, Charles J. Noke was never satisfied. After secretly experimenting for four years with a glaze using a compound of the metal titanium, Noke assembled an entire team of chemists, potters, and artists to transform his ideas into a viable commodity.

Before the Titanian Wares were perfected, a stronger, translucent body had to be created. Existing glazes and ceramic pigments had to be altered to adhere to this newly designed body. Artists closely associated with the development of the Titanian Wares were Robert Allen, Harry Allen, Harry Tittensor, and Harry Nixon.

In 1915 Titanian pieces were introduced to the ceramic market. Favorably received by critics in the press, they were described in the *British Architect*, May 1915, as "another charming ware of great refinement." The new glaze further established Noke's reputation as an extraordinary talent in the ceramic world. Each piece glowed with an ethereal quality in pastel colors of mottled greens, blues, and grays, which created their soft, cloudy appearance.

Some of the vases were glazed with such depth and clarity that they give the illusion of being filled with water. Many of the wares had no hand-painted decoration, but achieved their effects through the subtle colors gliding across simple shapes. On the smaller, more delicate pieces, the new body was as fine as ancient Chinese porcelain.

Many Titanian pieces directly reflect the make-believe kingdom of Oberon and Titania. Gnomes, birds, Oriental subjects, and even polar bears appeared on these vases. A number of figures, among them Buddhas, spooks, and gnomes were also produced in the Titanian body and glaze.

Varieties of Titanian also combined flambé and Chang effects. Rarer examples included raised gold and silver rims with enamel embellishments designed by Robert Allen and executed by Doulton's finest gilders.

Production was practically discontinued by 1925, although a few pieces were supplied for special orders in the early 1930s. Titanian's short ten-year production period (1915-1925) yielded more than fifty shapes and sizes of vases and bowls as well as a limited number of figures – each one an example of Charles J. Noke's gift to the world of collectibles.

Pair of Titanian duck vases, 1919. Harry Allen, artist. Royal Doulton backstamp, 6". (C)

Titanian owl vase with mice, c. 1905. Artist unknown.
Doulton England backstamp, 10". (T)

Two Titanian vases, one with a bird and one with swans, c. 1910.
Harry Allen, artist. Royal Doulton backstamp, 8.75", 2.75". (B ea.)

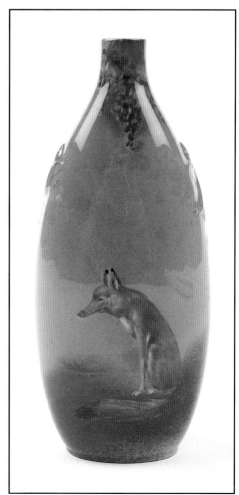

Titanian fox vase, c. 1916.
Harry Allen, artist. Royal
Doulton backstamp, 7". (C)

Titanian peacock pitcher, c. 1905. Artist unknown. Doulton England backstamp, 9.25". (*D*)

Titanian peacock vase, c. 1900. Artist unknown. Doulton England backstamp, 13.5". (*D*)

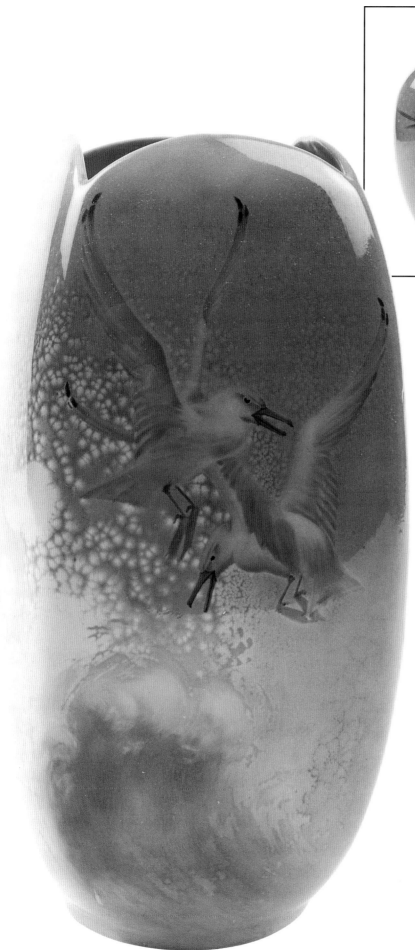

Titanian bird (left) and Night Heron, 1921. Bird:
F. Henri, artist; Night heron: Harrry Allen, artist.
4.5" ea. (C)

Titanian bird vase, c. 1920. Harry Allen, artist. Royal
Doulton backstamp, 7". (B)

Titanium vase with birds in flight over ocean wave,
c. 1920. Harry Allen, artist. Royal
Doulton backstamp, 8". (B)

Titanian swan vase, 1920. Harry Allen, artist. Royal Doulton England backstamp, 15.5". (C)

Titanian swan vase, 1920. F. Henri, artist. Royal Doulton England backstamp, 5". (C)

Titanian duck vase, c. 1905. Artist unknown. Doulton England backstamp, 10". (C)

Titanian pig with silver rim, c. 1920. Artist unknown. Royal Doulton England backstamp, 3". (C)

Titanian lop-eared rabbit, 1920. Artist unknown. Royal Doulton England backstamp, 4". (B)

Titanian dish with grotesque figure on top, c. 1920. Artist unknown. Royal Doulton backstamp, 5". (C)

Titanian grotesque figure on rock, c. 1916. Artist unknown. Royal Doulton backstamp, 4". (C)

Titanian vase with mandarin figure attached, c. 1915. Charles J. Noke, designer; Harry Allen, artist. (*H*)

Titanian butterfly jar and lid, c. 1920. Artist unknown. Royal Doulton England backstamp, 2.5" (B)

Titanian vase of Asian woman, c. 1905. Harry Tittensor, artist. Royal Doulton backstamp, 8". (C)

Titanian polar bear vase, c. 1916. Artist unknown. Royal Doulton Titanian backstamp, 7.5". (C)

Chinese Jade

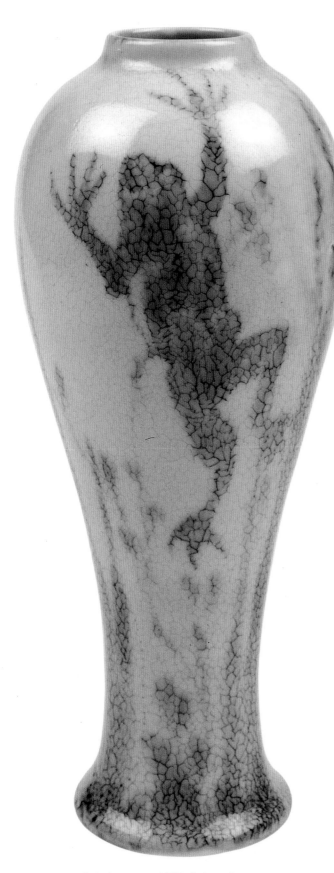

Jade frog vase, 1927. Artist unknown.
Royal Doulton England
backstamp, 7.5". (C)

Jade pair of cockatoos, 1931. Charles J. Noke and Harry Nixon, artists.
Royal Doulton England backstamp, 4.5". (C)

Pair of Jade vases, c. 1920. Charles J. Noke and Harry Nixon,
artists. Chinese Jade Royal Doulton backstamp, 10". (B)

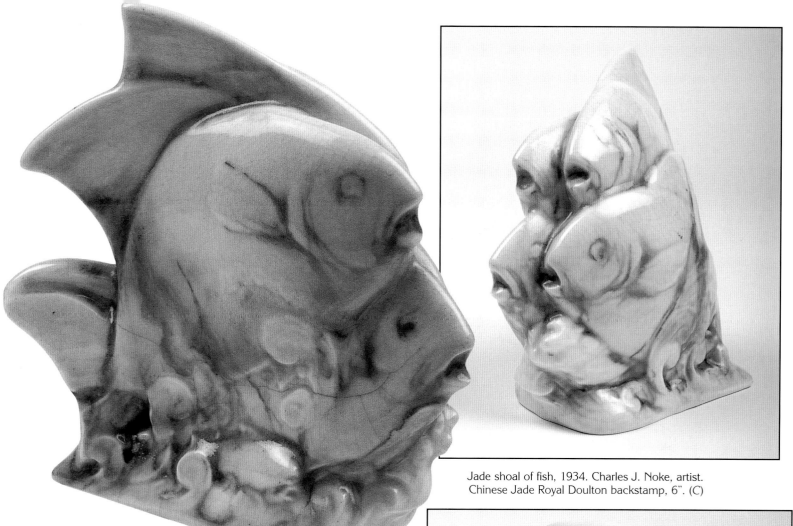

Jade shoal of fish, 1934. Charles J. Noke, artist. Chinese Jade Royal Doulton backstamp, 6". (C)

Jade Bonzo dog, c. 1920. Charles J. Noke, artist. Doulton England backstamp, 2". (T)

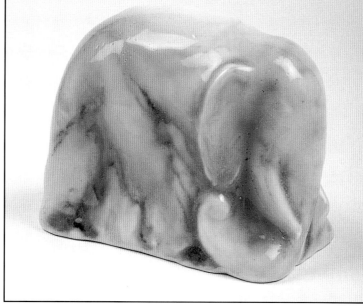

Jade elephant, 1930. Charles J. Noke and Harry Nixon, artists. Chinese Jade Royal Doulton backstamp, 3". (C)

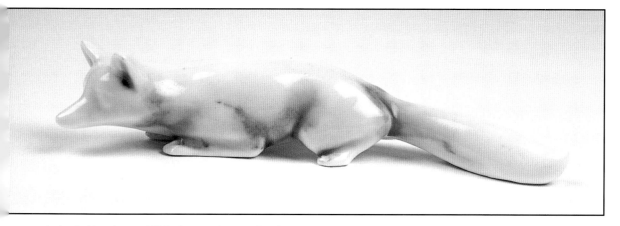

Jade slinking fox, c. 1920. Artist unknown. Doulton England backstamp, 8.5". (B)

Experimental Glazes

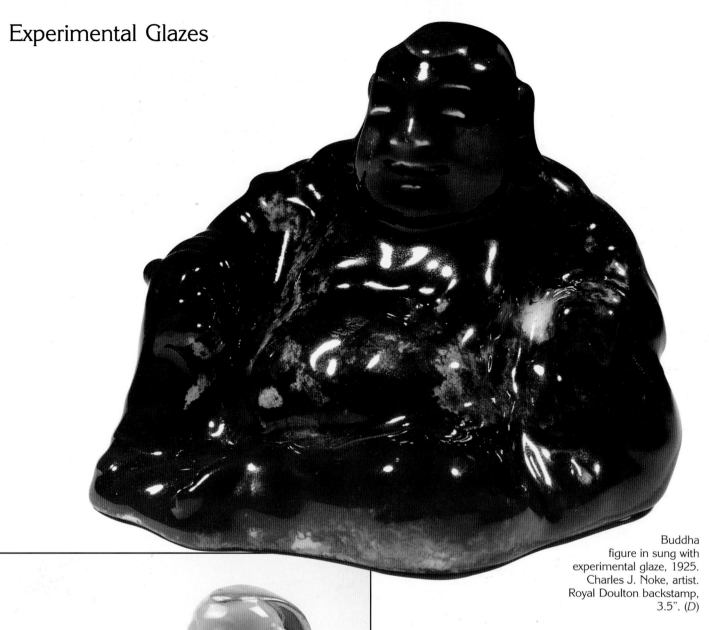

Buddha figure in sung with experimental glaze, 1925. Charles J. Noke, artist. Royal Doulton backstamp, 3.5". (*D*)

Buddha figure in experimental glaze, c. 1925. Charles J. Noke, artist. Royal Doulton backstamp, 4". (*D*)

Polar bears on ice in experimental glaze, c. 1912. Artist unknown. Royal Doulton backstamp, 3". (*C*)

Fox in experimental glaze, c. 1915. Artist unknown. Royal Doulton backstamp, 5.75". (B)

Penguins in experimental glaze, c. 1920. Artist unknown. Royal Doulton backstamp, 7". (A)

Polar bear in experimental glaze, 1935. Artist unknown. Royal Doulton backstamp, 4.5". (C)

Pig group in experimental glaze, c. 1925. Charles J. Noke, artist. Royal Doulton backstamp, 2". (A)

Bibliography and Additional Reading

Atterbury, Paul and Louise Irvine. *The Doulton Story*. Stoke on Trent, England: Royal Doulton Tableware Limited, 1979.

Betteridge, Margaret, *Royal Doulton Exhibition 1979*. Sydney, Australia: Museum of Applied Arts and Sciences, 1979.

Eyles, Desmond. *Royal Doulton 1815-1965; The Rise and Expansion of the Royal Doulton Potteries*. London, England: Hutchinson and Company, LTD., 1965.

_____. *The Doulton Burslem Wares*. London, England: Barries and Jenkins LTD., 1980.

Eyles, Desmond, Louise Irvine, and Valerie Baynton. *Royal Doulton Figures*. Somerset, London: Richard Dennis, 1994.

Eyles, Desmond and Louise Irvine. *The Doulton Lambeth Wares*. Somerset, England: Richard Dennis, 2002.

Lukins, Jocelyn. *Doulton for the Collector*. Burton upon Trent, England: PWC Publishing. (No Date)

_____. *Doulton Lambeth Advertising Wares*. (No City Listed) Venta Books, 1990.

McKeown, Julie. *Royal Doulton*. Buckinghamshire, England: Shire Publications Ltd., 1998.

Queree, Jennifer. *Royal Doulton*. Christchurch, New Zealand: Canterbury Museum, 1993.

Rose, Peter. *Hannah Barlow: A Doulton Artist*. London, England: Richard Dennis, 1985.

_____. *George Tinworth*. Los Angeles, California: C.D.N. Corporation, 1982.

Guide to Value Codes

A	$800-1500
B	$1501-2000
C	$2501-3000
D	$3001-4000
E	$4001-5000
F	$5001-5500
G	$5501-6000
H	$6001-7000
I	$7001-8000
J	$8001-9000
K	$9001-10000
L	$10001-11000
M	$11001-12000
N	$12001-14000
O	$14001-16000
P	$16001-18000
Q	$18001-22000
R	$22001-25000
S	$25001-30000
T	Unknown

Pulpit sculpted by George Tinworth for the Philadelphia Centennial Exhibition, 1876.

US $95.00

9 780764 317972   59500

ISBN: 0-7643-1797-0